FROM BALLOTS TO BREADLINES

AMERICAN WOMEN
1920-1940

THE YOUNG OXFORD HISTORY OF WOMEN IN THE UNITED STATES

Nancy F. Cott, *General Editor*

FROM BALLOTS TO BREADLINES

AMERICAN WOMEN 1920-1940

Sarah Jane Deutsch

OXFORD UNIVERSITY PRESS

New York • Oxford

To my grandmother, Pearle Catsman Dubois, who came of age in the 1920s, and to her buoyant, adventurous spirit

Oxford University Press

Oxford New York Toronto
Delhi Bombay Calcutta Madras Karachi
Kuala Lumpur Singapore Hong Kong Tokyo
Nairobi Dar es Salaam Cape Town
Melbourne Auckland Madrid
and associated companies in
Berlin Ibadan

Copyright © 1994 by Sarah Jane Deutsch

Introduction copyright © 1994 by Oxford University Press, Inc.

Published by Oxford University Press, Inc., 200 Madison Avenue, New York, New York 10016

Oxford is a registered trademark of Oxford University Press, Inc.

Library of Congress Cataloging-in-Publication Data

Deutsch, Sarah
From ballots to breadlines: American Women, 1920–1940 / Sarah Jane Deutsch.
p. cm. — (The Young Oxford history of women in the United States ; v. 8)
Includes bibliographical references and index.
ISBN 0-19-508063-7
ISBN 0-19-508830-1 (series)
1. Women—United States—History—20th century—Juvenile literature 2. Women—United States—Social conditions—
Juvenile literature [1. Women—History. 2. Women—Social conditions. 3. United States—Social conditions.]
I. Title II. Series.
HQ1420.D48 1994
305.4'0973—dc20   93-30664
                                                                        CIP
                                                                        AC

1 3 5 7 9 8 6 4 2
Printed in the United States of America
on acid-free paper

Design: Leonard Levitsky
Layout: Loraine Machlin
Picture research: Lisa Kirchner, Laura Kreiss

On the Cover: Office Girls by Raphael Soyer (1936), oil on canvas, 26 x 24 inches (66cm x 61cm). Collection of Whitney Museum of American Art. Purchase 36.149.
Frontispiece: U.S. Representatives Alice Mary Robertson, Mae Ella Nolan, and Winifred Huck (left to right) in front of the Capitol in 1923. All Republicans, they represented Oklahoma, California, and Illinois, respectively.

CONTENTS

INTRODUCTION

T he interwar period (between World Wars I and II) pre-
sents great contrasts. The 1920s (the Roaring Twenties) is usually seen as a decade of prosperity and frivolity abruptly ended by the Great Depression, which
lasted through the 1930s. In national politics, the Republican-domi-
nated stasis of the 1920s gives way to the Democratic activism of
the New Deal. From the perspective of women's history, however,
there are some important continuities between the two decades, both
equally part of a new era of mass culture and mass consumption
that shaped gender roles. New media—radio and movies—and mass
advertising, which was infused with social scientific expertise, invented new standards of beauty and femininity. Women's household and family roles were shaped by consumerism, through the
waxing and waning of prosperity and political administrations.

Moreover, a look into women's history makes the 1920s and
the 1930s each more difficult to characterize by the traditional standards. In the political history of women, 1920 is the great divide for
that is when, after many decades of campaigning, women were given
the vote nationally by the 19th Amendment to the Constitution. The
1920s, rather than simply a "return to normalcy" after World War
I, was a new era for women voters. It was one in which political
solidarity among women proved to be harder to mobilize than it

Ruth Hanna McCormick, shown here with her children, was a Republican representative in Congress from 1929 to 1931. She represented the state of Illinois.

had been during the struggle for enfranchisement, as this volume shows. If the 1920s was not all frivolity for American women, the 1930s was not all deprivation, either. Indeed, the new government initiatives of the New Deal (along with Eleanor Roosevelt's influential position as First Lady) provided unprecedented opportunities for women in political life and certain occupations, especially in social welfare. The many-sided meanings of the rise in women's employment during the 1930s are explored here.

This book is part of a series that covers the history of women in the United States from the 17th through the 20th century. Traditional historical writing has dealt almost entirely with men's lives because men have, until very recently, been the heads of state, the political officials, judges, ministers, and business leaders who have wielded the most visible and recorded power. But for several recent decades, new interest has arisen in social and cultural history, where common people are the actors who create trends and mark change as well as continuity. An outpouring of research and writing on women's history has been part of this trend to look at individuals and groups who have not held the reins of rule in their own hands but nonetheless participated in making history. The motive to address and correct sexual inequality in society has also vitally influenced women's history, on the thinking that knowledge of the past is essential to creating justice for the future.

The histories in this series look at many aspects of women's lives. The books ask new questions about the course of American history. How did the type and size of families change, and what difference did that make to people's lives? What expectations for women differed from those for men, and how did such expectations change over the centuries? What roles did women play in the economy? What form did women's political participation take when they could not vote? And how did politics change when women did gain full citizenship? How did women work with other women who were like or unlike them, as well as with men, for social and political goals? What sex-specific constraints or opportunities did they face? The series aims to understand the diverse women who have peopled American history by investigating their work and leisure, family patterns, political activities, forms of organization, and outstanding accomplishments. Standard events of American history, from the settling of the continent to the American Revolution, the Civil War, industrialization, the U.S. entry onto the world stage, and world wars, are all here, too, but seen from the point of view of women's experiences. Together, the answers to new questions and the treatment of old ones from women's points of view make up a compelling narrative of four centuries of history in the United States.

—Nancy F. Cott

The world of business offered new opportunities to women, as telephones and typewriters became standard office equipment. The ad above suggests that a woman's school should provide training not only in housekeeping, dressmaking, and laundry but also in the "business department."

THE YOUNG OXFORD HISTORY OF WOMEN IN THE UNITED STATES

CHAPTER 1

IMAGES AND LIVES

Our images of the 1920s, when we have images, are filled with young women with short hair and short skirts. They are kicking up their legs and kicking off a century of social restrictions. They smoke. They dance. They read racy literature. And they do it all in public. They have "advanced" ideas about sex, too. They have taken the socially outrageous, bohemian behavior of the previous generation's Greenwich Village set, and, to the horror of their parents, have brought it to Main Street.

What was going on with women in the 1920s and 1930s was, of course, more complicated than these images of "flappers." These images tend to be of young, white, middle-class women. There were African Americans, Chicanas, Asian Americans, and other women who aspired to be or were flappers, too, but most women of any race or ethnicity lived quite differently. Their lives, like our visions of the past, were affected by these images, but they did not mirror them. Although the 1920s did abound with flappers and would-be flappers, the decade also hosted mothers, professionals, women struggling in poverty, and women asserting new power.

There is another level on which images mattered in the 1920s. There was, above all, a pervasive sense of newness. To many it seemed that the world was made new after the massive destruction of World War I ended in 1918—and that women were made new too. What

A flapper with her roadster in 1926. The new woman behind the wheel of the newly cheap, mass-produced car signaled a new world where women might go anywhere, any time.

11

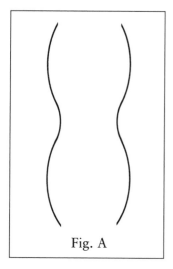

Fig. A

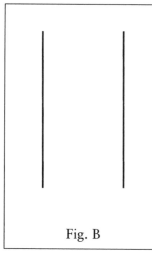

Fig. B

in fact was the "new" woman, this creature who, by 1920, could for the first time legally vote in national elections on the same basis as men everywhere in the United States? She was the result of competing desires, visions, and needs from a variety of sources. She looked different to different eyes.

When historians discuss such transformations, they like to talk about the way we, as a society, construct ideas about what a woman is. It is perhaps easiest to understand what historians mean by the social construction of womanhood by looking at the literal construction of woman.

Both of the figures on this page were literal constructions of women. That is, people created fashions that demanded a certain "look" from women, then designed clothing to create that look by shaping women's bodies in certain ways. Neither Figure A nor Figure B looks very much like women's own bodies. The first one, the 19th-century hourglass figure, took 25 pounds of pressure per square inch, in the form of tightly laced whalebone corsets, to create. The second one, the figure of the 1920s new woman, required breast binders and girdles, which were more comfortable, perhaps, but no more natural.

Why would anyone do this to women? The woman in Figure A could not breathe well with all that pressure and could not move freely without fainting. But women were not supposed to. That figure represented the ideal of 19th-century womanhood—a homebound, domestic creature unfit (thanks in part to corsets) for the rough world outside the home. She was a creature for a private world and a sign that her husband or father was making enough money to spare her any need to put forth physical effort.

Of course, women without such providers had to do a substantial amount of physical labor themselves. They could not wear tight, confining corsets. As a result, they were not seen by the upper classes as being "real" women; they were too free with their actions, too free with their bodies (no corsets), too free altogether.

On the other hand, in the 1920s the new woman, represented by those two straight lines in Figure B, was clearly the opposite. She was not a domestic woman. Like men of the day, she was a public figure, so her public figure would be like men's. But the reconstruction of the concept of "woman," of what it meant to be

female, even in the ideal, was not as easy as the reconstruction of fashion.

World War I had wrought dramatic changes in the United States, changes with vital implications for the lives of women. Although the war had begun in Europe in 1914, the United States had entered the conflict only in early 1917. Before the war, the federal government had confined itself to a relatively small range of activities. For example, it maintained a small army and a relatively small navy. It monitored exports and imports. It provided virtually no social services, rarely involved itself in relations between employers and employees, and professed a hands-off economic policy.

In its year and a half of active participation in World War I, the government vastly increased its armed forces, took over the running of the railroads and telephones, began some basic health services in remote rural areas, controlled prices for food and other commodi-

Three women prepare for a trip to California. The independent "new" women of the 1920s felt free not just to shorten their skirts but to abandon them. For the first time many women, like men, wore trousers.

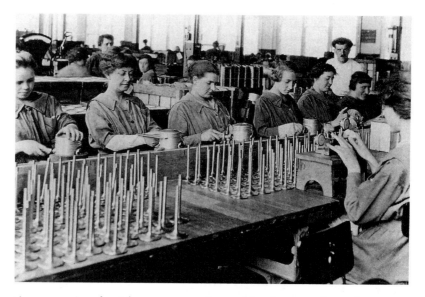

During World War I, companies often hired white women to replace male workers who had gone to fight. Here, women operate machinery and build motors on an assembly line at the Buick Motor Company (above) and the Lincoln Motor Company (right).

ties, negotiated with representatives of business and workers over working conditions and pay, created new government departments to look after the interests of women workers, and generally entered into the daily economic, social, and political lives of its citizens in newly intimate ways.

For many workers, the government was a far better boss than the private individuals who had been in charge of their lives. It paid better, set better hours, and was more responsive to their complaints. These and other workers faced the postwar world with increased expectations. They had worked hard. They had sacrificed for the war. They had been told they were fighting to save democracy. Now they expected a better world.

The war had also moved people around from place to place and job to job. As men of all races were called up to fight, companies that had previously hired only white men for well-paying jobs found themselves short of labor. For the first time, they began to hire white women and black men. Such jobs as streetcar conducting and railroad work paid more than these women had earned before. For black men, this was often their first chance to move from day labor or agricultural work into steadier, better-paying factory jobs.

Although some black women did manage to break into these newly available jobs, particularly on the railroad, for the most part the only jobs they found available were the ones white women had left. Even these jobs, even domestic service, in the North tended to pay better and offer better conditions than the ones southern African Americans could find at home. Ever since before the Civil War there had been a steady stream of black men and women leaving the South for the North. Now that stream became a torrent. At the same time, the United States made special arrangements with Mexico to bring Mexican workers across the border to work on railroads, in construction, and in harvesting. What began as wartime migrations continued throughout the 1920s.

All this movement brought new groups of people together and gave them new ways to think about their roles in society. There were racial tensions and sudden strikes by whites protesting the employment of blacks and by blacks protesting discrimination. Black women, whom whites were used to thinking of as quiet and obedient, threw down their tools and quit when foremen cursed at them for protesting conditions or when companies hired white women to supervise them. And white women and men also struggled over what

Many black women who worked were domestic servants. Few had been able to break into the industrial jobs that became available to white women and black men during the war years.

In Cincinnati, a cleaning woman prepares to scrub railroad cars. When black women did break into industrial jobs they got the least desirable ones.

their new working positions would mean after the war. The men of the Amalgamated Association of Street and Electric Railway Employees in New York City were so worried about the changes that they wrote a poem:

> We wonder where we are drifting, where is the freedom of the
>   stripes and stars
> If for the sake of greed and profit we put women conductors on
>   the cars
> When our dear brothers left us, shouldered their guns and went
>   to war,
> Little did we think street railway kings would use women like a
>   squaw.
> Woman is God's most tender flower, made to blossom and to
>   bear
> She was made by God the weaker, like a vine on man to lean
> She was meant to work like her nature, tender sweet and clean....
> We pray God to protect and keep women off the cars.

Many women had a different notion of their "nature," however. As if in answer to the men's poem, women machine tool workers retorted:

> The simple, tender, clinging vine,
> That once around the oak did twine
> Is something of the past;
> We stand now by your side
> And surmount obstacles with pride,
> We're equal, free at last
> And I would rather polish steel,
> Than get you up a tasty meal.

There had clearly been changes occurring during the war, and life would not be the same again. In October 1917, in New York City, the last great parade by women to gain the suffrage, the right to vote, included women factory workers and women doctors. After five victorious campaigns that year, women had full voting rights in 11 states (all west of the Mississippi, except New York) and Presidential suffrage in an additional 5. Women had been struggling and organizing to get the vote for at least 70 years. In 1918, President Woodrow Wilson finally declared himself in favor of a national woman suffrage amendment to the Constitution, declaring, "We have made partners of the women in this war." In 1919, the 19th Amendment had passed both houses of Congress, despite

National Guard troops patrol a Chicago neighborhood during the race riots of 1919, and police approach one of the victims (above).

solid southern opposition, and by August 1920 the amendment had been ratified.

But other expectations were not so easily met. In the two years after the war ended, the United States witnessed perhaps its greatest upheaval. In 1919 alone, 4 million workers, or one out of every five workers, went out on strike, and there were major race riots in 25 towns and cities, including Charleston, South Carolina; Washington, D.C.; and Chicago. In Chicago, 500 people were wounded, and 23 blacks and 15 whites were killed. The number of lynchings of black citizens, many of the victims still wearing their army uniforms, skyrocketed.

In April 1919, the women of the New England Union of Telephone Operators went on strike. Postmaster General Albert Burleson, who still retained his temporary wartime control over the telephone industry, refused to negotiate. He hired company spies to infiltrate the strikers' ranks and used armed force. What had started as a struggle over wages became a fight to defend the right to bargain collectively, that is, to gather as a group and negotiate with the owners of a business.

The women, though mostly inexperienced at striking, presented a solid front, and the male phone workers joined them. When Burleson

These mill workers from Lawrence, Massachusetts, went on strike in 1919. Employers' publicity and media attacks led many Americans to fear that such strikes were the result of communist infiltration and to support harsh measures against labor unions.

threatened to replace them with soldiers, 100 women picketers, accompanied by male relatives in uniform carrying military service flags, blocked their way. The disgusted soldiers said they had not expected to come home from the war to fight women. Nor would the Boston police arrest the strikers. Women doctors gave the strikers free medical care, and restaurant owners kept them fed. Burleson brought in scabs—nonunion strikebreakers—from out of town, but no one would serve them or work with them. The solidarity of the workers and community support brought the strikers victory in only five days.

Few other strikes, however, enjoyed similar success. When a general strike in Seattle peacefully shut down the city, the mayor called in the troops. In the steel industry, where more than half the common laborers were immigrants, employers played up an image of the strikers as foreign agitators. In the wake of the 1917 Russian Revolution and the creation of an international Communist party in 1919, the employers labeled the strikers radical revolutionaries.

To much of the public witnessing the strikes and riots, it did seem as though the United States was verging on revolution. Steel-plant employers succeeded in convincing federal agents to round up and deport thousands of immigrant strikers with no proof of wrong-doing, and the general public did not protest. This anti-Communist fever, known as the Red Scare, raged in 1919 and 1920. Americans watched in near silence as government agents invaded private homes and raided not just union offices but also the offices of dissenting political organizations, arrested and deported members, and destroyed records. They held people on false charges and denied them lawyers in the name of restoring order. No one who had ever raised a voice in protest was safe.

By the end of 1920, all was quiet. Yet no one could know what the future would hold. It was into this uneasy peace that the new woman would emerge.

In this political cartoon depicting the Red Scare, Labor and Capital fight on the dock while Bolshevikism steams into the harbor. In the water to the left, Prosperity is drowning.

CHAPTER 2

THE NATURE OF "LIBERATION": INVENTING A PUBLIC WOMAN

It was August 1920, and Tennessee's legislature was debating the national woman suffrage amendment. Tennessee's ratification would put the number of states needed to ratify the 19th Amendment over the top (the Constitution required approval by three-fourths of the state legislatures) and women across the country would have the right to vote. "It's hot, muggy, nasty, and this last battle is desperate," wrote Carrie Chapman Catt, leader of the main national woman suffrage organization. Mrs. Catt had arrived in Tennessee in July with an overnight bag and stayed five weeks to ensure victory.

Suffrage opponents threatened legislators with ruin if they voted for ratification, and suffragists like Catt haunted the railroad stations to make sure their male allies did not flee the town. According to one historian, it all came down to Harry Burn. He came from a rural district in east Tennessee where the political leaders opposed ratification. But he was the youngest member of the legislature, and his mother, a staunch suffragist, had written her son: "Hurrah! And vote for suffrage and don't keep them in doubt.... Don't forget to be a good boy and help Mrs. Catt put 'Rat' in Ratification." Thanks to Burn, the amendment carried, by a vote of 49 to 47. On August 26, 1920, the governor of Tennessee certified the state's ratification of the 19th Amendment. Catt declared, "We are

Carrie Chapman Catt rides in a suffrage parade in 1920 to celebrate the ratification of the woman suffrage amendment in Tennessee.

New York's Harlem Equal Rights League was one of many local organizations organized to promote woman suffrage.

no longer petitioners, we are not wards of the nation, but free and equal citizens."

After 70 years of ups and downs, of local victories but many defeats, suffragists had learned to work on a number of levels at once and to benefit from a loosely knit set of coalitions. They had campaigned door to door, organizing women into political parties precinct by precinct. They had dared to hold open-air meetings on street corners. They had organized vast parades. Some had chained themselves to the White House fence to protest fighting for democracy abroad when it was lacking at home. Others had lobbied senators and representatives in their chambers. Some had tried to bridge racial gulfs; others avoided them. Some had even argued for women's votes on racial and ethnic grounds, so that, with the help of native-born white women, native-born white voters could outnumber voters of color and immigrants. However, African-American women and Latinas had long fought for the vote as well. They occasionally could join organizations led by white women, but more often they had their own organizations. Suffragists came in every style, race, and ethnicity, and for this one moment, they came together in the largest women's movement up to that time.

And then, suddenly, it was over. What had the victory meant? By the end of the 1920s, this united power of American womanhood seemed scarcely visible. The promises of unity would not be met in succeeding decades. During the 1920s, the country moved from an era of intense, collective action by women on behalf of women to an era when women's groups had little visibility and limited validity in the eyes of most people. It was not clear whether gaining the vote had liberated women or whether liberation had changed its meaning.

Suffragists had argued for giving women the vote on a wide range of grounds, but there were two basic camps. One claimed that justice demanded that women, as humans equal to men, have equal rights. In 1892, Elizabeth Cady Stanton was a suffrage leader; her home state of New York assumed that as a married woman with children she had a husband voting for her interests. Mrs. Stanton disputed that idea in front of Congress. "The individuality of each human soul," she insisted, "the right of individual conscience and judgment; our republican idea of individual citizenship" all demanded that women "have the same rights as all other members [of the country], according to the fundamental principles of government."

By the second decade of this century, however, Stanton's argument was fading. Whereas Stanton and others had argued that women deserved the vote simply because, like men, they were fully adult citizens, other suffragists argued that women deserved the vote precisely because they were *not* like men. Men had led us into war and corrupt government; women would nurture us into a more peaceful, ordered existence. Women would vote political machines out of office, would further refine the social welfare agencies they had already helped establish in many cities, and would eradicate the traffic in liquor and prostitution. Some people called the argument that women's votes would benefit society expedient, claiming that suffragists used such an argument because it would not threaten prevailing views of womanhood and the differences between women and men.

With these arguments dominant, Americans had high expectations of woman suffrage. The world, they were convinced, would be a different place once women had the vote. After 1920, politicians began to respond more carefully to women's grievances.

For a time, it seemed safest to do so. Yoncalla, Oregon, woke up after the election of 1920 to a "feminist revolution," according to one journalist. In this town of 323 residents, men outnumbered women by almost two to one, but the *Literary Digest* reported that the women had "risen in their wrath, stirred by the alleged inefficiency of the municipal officials, and swept every masculine office-holder out of his job." The women of the town had worked in absolute secrecy, not even telling their brothers and husbands. Only the town's women were in on the secret, and they prevailed at the polls. Mrs. Mary Burt, a university graduate, was the new mayor. She had lived in Yoncalla for 40 years and had long been active in the community. Also elected to the town government was Mrs. Laswell, wife of the ousted mayor. The only thing Mr. Laswell and his assistants could find to tell the press was that they were "much surprised."

At the other end of the country, in Washington, D.C., a spate of legislative and other victories also greeted women. The women's peace

The all-female town council of Yoncalla, Oregon, with Mayor Mary Burt in the center, in 1920.

movement succeeded in getting the United States to host and participate in an international disarmament conference in 1921. The Cable Act of 1922 gave married women independent citizenship; no longer would women who married foreigners lose their United States citizenship. And the Women's Bureau of the federal government, created during the war to look after the interests of women workers, became a permanent part of the Department of Labor in 1920.

Women streamed into public office in the 1920s, the largest single increase in women's officeholding to that date, leveling off only after 1930. The Democrats and Republicans began to mandate equal representation of men and women on party committees. Altogether, these achievements covering peace, politics, labor, health care, and the home seemed to indicate a wide acceptance of women's significance in the public arena.

Yet by 1924 popular magazines were running articles (written by men) with such titles as "Is Woman Suffrage a Failure?" and "Women's Ineffective Use of the Vote." There were signs, even early on, that not all was going according to plan. The only woman in Congress in 1921, Alice Robertson, was an anti-suffragist. Women vastly increased their numbers in office, but the meaning of that increase must be set in a wider context. In 1924, there were 84 women legislators in 30 states. Five years later there were 200, an increase of almost 250 percent. But while there were 200 women in office, there were 10,000 men. The numbers were similar at other levels of government. In New Jersey, for example, only 19 of 788 county officeholders were women. At the federal level, there were just 10 women in Congress in 1926; that year only two women were reelected to Congress in their own right, and only one was elected without the benefit of having completed a dead family member's term. The gains women sought could obviously not rely on strength at the top.

Political parties were reluctant to nominate women for offices that mattered. After arguing for so long that they were above politics, that they were interested in human welfare, not part of self-serving party political machines, women would have to prove to the men controlling political parties that they knew how to play the game. They had to prove that they could be loyal to the party and not just to principles. They had to prove that they represented a separate constituency, a group of voters they could mobilize to support them.

But women did not vote as a block. The fragments that had come together for the suffrage fight once more went their separate ways. As the 1920s wore on without the appearance of a solid block of women voters, an increasing number of delegations of women came to party conventions, only to have the party leaders pay less and less attention to them. At the 1924 Democratic convention, there were 180 women delegates and 239 women alternates. Eleanor Roosevelt, long active in politics and social welfare, headed a subcommittee to gather suggestions from women's organizations for planks on social welfare. But, as she recalled in her autobiography, *This Is My Story*, at the convention itself the women "stood outside the door of all important meetings and waited." Their turn never seemed to come.

Some activist women had long foreseen that the right to vote would not be a miracle cure for social ills, including the inferior status of women. Rose Schneiderman, an activist for the rights of working women, declared of the vote, "Men had it all these years and nothing of great importance had happened." The population in general, men as well as women, seemed to echo her disillusionment. Smaller and smaller percentages of those eligible

Alice Mary Robertson (top), a Republican, represented Oklahoma in Congress from 1921 to 1923. Below, congressional candidate Ruth Bryan Owen stands between her driver and her secretary during a campaign trip in Florida in 1929.

President Calvin Coolidge (front row, fourth from left) meets with Chamber of Commerce representatives in 1924. His Republican administration was filled with millionaire businessmen.

to vote did so. The number had been declining since 1896, when it had peaked at 79 percent. In 1912, before the passage of the woman suffrage amendment, only 59 percent of all people eligible to vote did so. By 1920, the number had sunk to 49 percent.

At the same time, government officials and most of those who elected them were retreating from a vision of government as an instrument to change society. They looked instead to a government that would restore law and order and protect business. They cared more about assisting employers than protecting the welfare of employees and the unemployed.

The Republicans held the Presidency throughout the 1920s. Calvin Coolidge, who became President when Warren Harding died in 1923, believed in business and in businessmen. He stocked his cabinet with businessmen and made them at home in the Republican party. As their money poured into Republican coffers, protective tariffs, or taxes on imports, on industrial goods rose and the courts made it harder for workers to strike. The *Wall Street Journal* happily announced, "Never before, here or anywhere else, has a government been so completely fused with business."

The new attitudes were reflected in the rulings of the courts, as they consistently overturned two decades of reform legislation aimed at regulating business, such as laws setting maximum hours or minimum wages for women. This was a time when there was no federal minimum-wage or maximum-hour law. Male and female workers simply struck the best bargain they could with their employers. Often they worked 12-hour days, 6 or 7 days a week. Often they earned only enough to provide them with food and shelter. If workers belonged to strong unions, they could get better conditions. Most unions, however, organized only skilled workers, and even among those unions, few organized women workers. Most women lacked the resources, education, or skills to have a strong bargaining position on their own.

Faced with these realities of vulnerable women in poor conditions, reformers looked to the government for a remedy. They recognized that only the government could set uniform minimum standards that would cover working women. The courts had always struck down such protective legislation for men, on the grounds that it interfered with men's freedom to make their own bargains. But in 1908, the Supreme Court, in *Muller* v. *Oregon*, decided to distinguish between men and women. In part, the Supreme Court argued that women were potential mothers of future citizens, so the government had a special interest in their well-being. The *Muller* ruling opened the way for legislation that would protect women's working conditions.

By 1923, 40 states regulated the hours of women's work, and 15 states as well as the District of Columbia regulated their wages. But two years earlier, an unemployed female worker had petitioned the federal district court for the District of Columbia to keep the minimum wage board of Washington, D.C., from enforcing its decisions on wages for women. She claimed that such enforcement had cost her a job. The Children's Hospital also brought action to prevent the minimum wage board and the board's chairman, Jesse C. Adkins, from forcing the hospital to pay higher wages. The case went to the Supreme Court on appeal. When it decided the case,

The National League of Women Voters called for government to pay attention to child welfare, women's working conditions, and public health. Maud Wood Park (right) was the League's first president.

Adkins v. *Children's Hospital,* in 1923, the Supreme Court struck down the Washington, D.C., minimum wage law for women. By doing so, it threatened all the protective legislation that progressive politicians and citizens had fought for and won in the previous 20 years.

The Supreme Court ruled that minimum wage boards were an arbitrary government interference in private affairs, infringing on freedom of contract. Justice George Sutherland, writing for the majority of the justices, struck over and over at what he considered false distinctions between women and men. Women, he declared, "are legally as capable of contracting for themselves as men." Giving women the vote had, according to Sutherland, eradicated differences in the civil status of men and women. With that in mind, he concluded that the law was unfair to the employer, "compelling him to pay not less than a certain sum . . . irrespective of the ability of his business to sustain the burden." Sutherland's claim regarding

Women factory workers assemble musical instrument cases and covers in 1927. Although the Supreme Court ruled in 1908 that legislation could regulate women's working conditions, in 1923 it struck down a minimum wage law for women.

women's equality with men was particularly ironic given the vast number of inequalities that remained embedded in the laws of the states and in the practices of governments as well as private corporations. Among other restraints, women found certain jobs legally closed to them, companies legally paid them less than men for the same work, some states barred them from serving on juries, and most states denied them equal access to credit, the right to borrow money.

To some triumphant suffragists the next logical step was an equal rights amendment, which would sweep away all remaining forms of discrimination at once. Activist Alice Paul spearheaded the drive for the Equal Rights Amendment (ERA). She presided over the National Women's Party (NWP) when in November 1923, the 75th anniversary of the first women's rights convention, at Seneca Falls, New York, it announced the text of the ERA: "Men and women shall have equal rights throughout the United States and every place subject to its jurisdiction." A month later the amendment was introduced into Congress.

To Paul, it was logical that the ERA should succeed suffrage as the focus of the NWP. Like suffrage, the ERA was only part of the feminist agenda, but it would give women power, which they could then use as they pleased.

Instead of becoming the new mass women's movement, however, the NWP dwindled. It emerged from the suffrage fight in 1920 with 35,000 members. By the end of the decade, it had sunk to 1,000. The problem lay partly in the tactics of the party. It neglected the local precinct-by-precinct organizing that had helped suffrage succeed. Instead it recruited highly visible celebrities, such as the artist Georgia O'Keeffe, the writer Edna St. Vincent Millay, and the aviator Amelia Earhart. But because they were symbolic of women's advances rather than representative of most women's lives, these women could not help broaden the base for a mass movement.

There were other problems as well. Crystal Eastman supported the Equal Rights Amendment but found it too narrow. A labor lawyer, social investigator, and the first female member of New York's Employer's Liability Commission, Eastman had written in 1918, "Life is a big battle for the complete feminist."

Alice Paul (right) shakes hands with Alva Belmont, who donated the headquarters of the National Woman's Party in Washington, D.C.

For someone like Eastman, the ERA was not the ultimate solution to women's inequality. It touched only on legal issues, not on social relations. It neither affected such concerns as birth control nor required a change in the social roles of men and women in the family. Referring to the National Woman's Party convention that had adopted the ERA, Eastman wrote, "If some such [broader] program could have been exhaustively discussed at that convention we might be congratulating ourselves that the feminist movement had begun in America. As it is all we can say is that the suffrage movement is ended."

The ERA's narrowness was particularly evident in regard to race. Alice Paul tried to ensure that the NWP, unlike some other suffrage groups, did not discriminate on the grounds of race. In 1921, the party encouraged black women to attend its national convention as delegates and speak there. But when Addie Hunton,

Members of the building committee insert a time capsule in the cornerstone of the YWCA's South Figueroa branch in Los Angeles. In the 1920s, many branches of the YWCA were segregated, but increasing pressure led to policy changes in many northern branches by the end of the decade.

a field secretary for the National Association for the Advancement of Colored People (NAACP), led a delegation of 60 black women from 14 states asking Paul to throw the party's energy into fighting against southern regulations and terrorism that kept black women as well as men from voting, Paul refused. That, she insisted, was a racial issue, not a women's issue. Paul drew a distinction between racial and sexual injustice that African-American women could not make in their daily lives.

Black women grew increasingly impatient with organizations, from the NWP to the Young Women's Christian Association (YWCA), that insisted they patiently wait until the nation was ready for further progress. They turned to their own organizing. Lugenia Hope had led Atlanta's Neighborhood Union during World War I when it had teamed up with the newly formed Atlanta Colored Women's War Council to further the war effort. The Neighborhood Union organized each neighborhood to work for community betterment in education, morals, food conservation, employment, health, housing, and entertainment. By 1922, its campaigns had resulted in streets being paved, sewers installed, houses repaired, and classes given on health, wages, and citizenship. Two years earlier, Hope had written Eva Bowles at the national YWCA board, demanding that "full recognition of leadership be given Negro women."

In September 1922, Mrs. Robert M. Patterson, a black socialist candidate for Pennsylvania's General Assembly, declared in the newspaper *Women's Voice:* "Never was there a time in which there was greater need for sane and sober thought on the part of Negro women. . . . We need women who will not sell their rights for a mess of pottage. . . . We must not permit the fight for equal civil rights to cease until it will be possible for every citizen, without regard to race, to have complete civil rights granted to him or her."

However, white women even quarreled among themselves over what civil rights for women meant. At the very moment when Florence Kelley, a social reformer and activist, was marshaling her forces to try to avert the overturn of protective legislation in the *Adkins* case, the NWP submitted a brief on the other side. It was, after all, an unemployed woman who was co-petitioner against the minimum wage for women.

Lugenia Hope led Atlanta's Neighborhood Union during the war in order to improve city services for black neighborhoods.

The Women's Trade Union League included working women in its leadership. The letterhead indicates which union each official represents.

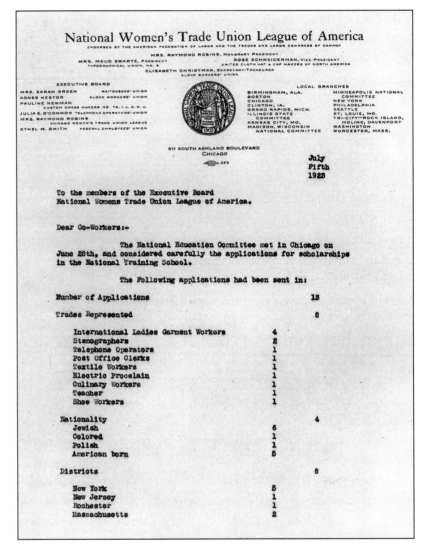

In the NWP, Paul and Eastman both had worked closely with working women. They now believed that protective legislation, not just for the minimum wage but also laws against women working at night, prevented women from getting the most lucrative jobs and justified persistent inequalities. On the other hand, Florence Kelley had as allies the Women's Trade Union League, an organization partly made up of and led by wage-earning women. To them, protective legislation acknowledged the realities of unequal social and economic power; the ERA did not. If woman suffrage could produce the kind of damage evident in Justice Sutherland's argument, the ERA seemed to them even more potentially damaging in his hands. Caught by the reality of women's diverse social and economic situations and needs, women divided instead of uniting over the ERA and protective legislation.

But the divisions among women were not all caused by the women themselves. For one thing, the raids and prosecutions of the Red Scare had a chilling effect on women's groups. Facing possible jail terms or deportation simply for associating with radical women, some women turned a cold shoulder to former friends. In an era in which organizing at all was suspect, women in the 1920s could either organize together for equality and rights and be labeled "red" and fired, or they could try to go it alone.

It was not then surprising that women in their 20s and 30s who wanted to succeed in the public world of business or politics believed the most important thing to leave behind was "sex-consciousness," their sense of themselves as women who shared interests with other women. They abandoned any organized quest for general social reform and opted instead for individualism. "Breaking into the human race," as they put it, and individual success in the world as it was became their goals.

In 1927, journalist Dorothy Dunbar Bromley wrote in "Feminist—New Style," in *Harper's*. "The pioneer feminists were hard-hitting individuals, and the modern young woman admires them for their courage," Bromley admitted, "even while she judges them for their zealotry and their inartistic methods." "They fought her battle," according to Bromley, "but *she* does not want to wear their mantle."

These women wanted to emancipate themselves from each other, from their families, and from the assumption that women were more virtuous than men and more responsible for social welfare. For them, individuality became a way to allow for diversity among women, and it would lead to models of individual accomplishment. It would not, however, lead to the betterment of the group.

Moreover, this rejection of an older style of feminism and virtuous womanhood came at a time when there was not yet an alternative with which to replace it. In opting to make it in a man's world without changing that world, these women had to try to become like men. Feminists had not yet succeeded in creating a third category, though they desired it, of the "human" sex. Even when coa-

Women meet for a Tuesday afternoon art club, sponsored by the Bureau of Recreation in Pittsburgh.

litions of women formed to support the ERA, they did it, they claimed, so that they could be treated "just like men."

Despite antagonism toward feminist groups, the 1920s found activist women not so much absent as scattered. No longer were they the "woman movement," as they had been in the 19th century; now they were women. They still organized, but in a multitude of smaller groups that often opposed each other. Every woman seemed to belong to at least one group, and often to several. There were church groups, parents' associations, self-improvement clubs, and civic leagues. Many women returned to the causes that had most concerned them before the peak of the suffrage movement. Some threw all their efforts into the peace movement. Others returned to such issues as social reform, hours and wages for women, clean city streets and water, adequate schooling and playgrounds, and safe factory conditions, for example. In the South, new interracial efforts against lynching occupied some women. In the Southwest, some Hispanic women worked for bilingual education.

Still other women lobbied for their professional interests. The members of Business and Professional Women, founded in 1918, had originally promoted a broad program to make marriage and divorce laws the same in all states, to gain higher status for home economics in federal aid to state education, and to pass laws regu-

Uniformed members of the Regina Mothers Club of Pittsburgh meet for a gym class in 1926.

lating the use of child labor. In the 1920s, they increasingly focused on their own interests as professional women and office workers. All this activity, though scattered, was still movement.

The 1920s represented a new era for women. The vote had not given them equal rights or opportunities. But it had, along with postwar politics, brought change. The decade of the 1920s found women struggling to find a new language, and new strategies appropriate to their new context.

In Evanston, Illinois, leaders from business and professional women's clubs gather for the state meeting in 1925.

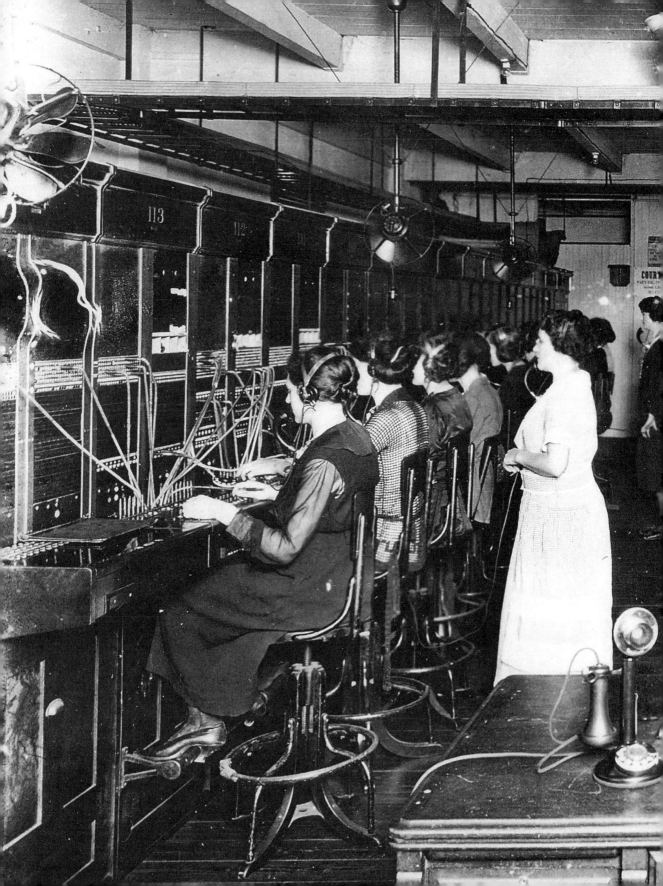

CHAPTER 3

WOMEN'S WORK

I n 1921, a Chicago telephone operator reported the inside scoop on her job to the Women's Trade Union League paper, *Life and Labor*. She found the phone company to be not just an employer but a nosy and demanding parent. When she had applied to the company, she had had to undergo a medical examination and take psychological tests and answer such questions as whether she lived with her husband and whether he objected to her working. She spent three weeks in training, during which gum chewing was strictly forbidden. The classes taught more than how to handle telephone equipment; they also instructed operators how to talk. She learned to reply to callers with a particular singsong set of phrases. Unshakably polite, musical tones were required.

When not in classes, and later, on their breaks, the telephone operators could enjoy the company's recreation room. It had comfortable couches and chairs, reading lamps, magazines, a piano, and a record player. It also had spotlessly clean, spacious bathrooms with lots of large mirrors and all the modern conveniences. Moreover, the company provided free lunches, free medical service, and reduced prices for theater tickets and groceries. It did not pay wages as high as work that required less education and less expensive clothing, and placed fewer restrictions on language and behavior, but the operator wrote that few of the girls would complain. Few of the other workers seemed to share her opinion that "those of us who retain any sense of independence and self-respect would prefer to

A supervisor monitors the operators of the Southern Telephone and Telegraph Company in 1921.

Women eat lunch in the women's lunchroom of the United Shoe Machinery Company in Beverly, Massachusetts (above); others relax in a lounge at the Gibson Art Company in Cincinnati. Many businesses felt that providing such "enforced recreation," away from men, would improve the lives and work of their female employees.

have our salaries large enough so that we could pay for our own lunches and medical service."

This description encapsulates much about women's paid work in the 1920s. To begin with, as a married woman, this particular operator had plenty of company. The percentage of wives working for pay soared in the decade, especially among those aged 20 to 35. But this shift was not matched by a change in attitudes toward women. One national advice columnist claimed that the question she was asked most frequently was, "Should a woman work outside the home after marriage?" despite the fact that increasing numbers of women were already doing so. By 1930, 40 percent of white and black working women were wives, one-third with children under age 13, but they still constituted only 11.7 percent of all wives. Several states still banned married women from holding government jobs. Though the percentage of married women teachers doubled, the majority of school boards refused to hire them.

Many people were worried about what it would mean to have wives work outside the home. What concerned them most was what it would mean to have white married women working outside the home. Black married women had long been forced by economic necessity to work for wages, and among agricultural worker families, 60 percent of Chicanas with children worked in the fields. Japanese immigrant women had been partners in their husbands' businesses, domestic servants in other people's homes, and agricultural laborers ever since their arrival in large numbers between 1907 and 1921. Married Puerto Rican women in New York City contracted with textile manufacturers to make garments, fine lace, and other goods in their homes. The press and policymakers had never worried about what those women's work would do to their families. It was only when non-Hispanic, white native-born or even immigrant married women began to work outside the home in larger numbers that the issue became a public one.

This sort of concern meant that the work that married white women, or marriageable white women, did had to be seen as compatible with older notions of what was proper womanly behavior. For instance, a telephone operator, if married, had to have her husband's permission to work. She had to dress with decorum and maintain a sweet temperament. Indeed, it was the very assumption that women were by nature sweet and submissive that the telephone company used to justify hiring women as operators to begin with. The company then converted this assumption into fact by training its employees to sound sweet and submissive on the phone and firing those who did not.

The telephone industry formed just one part of an expanding service sector in the 1920s. New forms of communication and new business technologies, such as typing and stenography, vastly increased the number of clerical jobs available. Men had dominated clerical work in the 19th century, but as businesses hired more and more typists and clerks relative to the number of managers, typing and clerking stopped being routes to the top in most firms. As such jobs became dead-end, fewer men and more women wound up in clerical positions. Clerical work thus became a larger and larger proportion of the posts women held, outdistancing domestic service (previously the largest sector), teaching, and industrial jobs. By 1930, 2 million women, or one-fifth of the female labor force, were office workers.

As more women came to hold these positions, the jobs became redefined. The secretary was no longer the man on the rise, but the

Since well before the 1920s, married immigrant women, like this Japanese field worker, had toiled along with their husbands in order for their families to survive.

Women take the Wisconsin state civil service exam in 1918. Women increasingly dominated clerical and secretarial work in the 1920s.

office wife, radiating sunshine and sympathy. Women uneasy about becoming mannish by being on male terrain helped along the redefinition. They wore unbusinesslike clothes—soft and stylish dresses, for example. For the men in management, redefining clerical workers made women less threatening by clearly distinguishing their separate roles. Clerical work, previously a man's job, became "women's work," something requiring a "woman's touch."

There were still tensions in the workplace. Women's increasing dominance of clerical positions came at the same time that businesses were enlarging. As women got stuck in low-paying office jobs, men could now get stuck in middle management, without much freedom to do the job as they wished. Men felt hemmed in and blamed their new office wives. For their part, secretaries found men they worked for moody, difficult, and irrational. Grace Robinson, a former secretary, complained to the readers of *Liberty* in 1928 that "the man one works for has, more than likely, a healthy, well nourished temper that all its life has been permitted to cavort about naked, untrammeled, and undisciplined." Male bosses began to prefer their female office workers to have only a high school, not a college, degree and to be young enough that the term *girl* could become just another word for *clerical worker*. Youth and education would make the hierarchy in the office clearer. By the decade's end, this equation was so thoroughly cemented that no matter how old the secretary was, she was still a girl to her boss.

It was not only in the "girlishness" of telephone operators that they typified some aspects of the 1920s. Part of the appeal of telephone work undoubtedly lay in the well-appointed lounge. At the turn of the century, young working women had most often lived at home or as boarders with other families. Now, between school and marriage they lived in their own apartments. They often shared these apartments with other young working women. Having their own apartments gave them a sense of autonomy, of young adulthood, of being unsupervised and unrestrained. It gave their parents a lot of worry.

At the same time, young working women hardly lived in the lap of luxury. At $15 a week, their wages supported only tiny, often ill-lit apartments with sparse furnishings. For women doing dull work and living in dingy, dark apartments on boring, cheap food, the phone company's lounge and benefits gave them as close a glimpse as they might ever have of the middle-class world many wanted. Whenever they sought more from life, to take in the new movies or go to amusement parks, or have a decent dinner, they had to find a man, who was better paid, to treat them. Young working women had started dating men to whom they had not been introduced, without supervision, almost a generation earlier. By the 1920s, this practice was widespread.

Lounges, theater tickets, and lunches formed part of the new strategies by which large corporations had responded to the massive number of strikes in 1919. Many adopted something called the American Plan of corporate welfare. Instead of paying higher wages, companies provided increased benefits to workers. For example, some companies offered subsidized housing or loans. Such benefits made it harder for workers to leave the company, no matter what the conditions of the work itself, and they were less likely to risk losing their benefits by striking.

Only large companies could afford such programs, and most women who worked in industry worked for smaller firms. Women of color, in particular, rarely found such enlightened employers. During World War I, half a million black southerners moved to northern cities. More followed them after the war. They thought they were heading toward the Promised Land, where they could work as well as vote on equal terms with whites. Mothers labored outside the home so that their daughters could stay in high school long enough to qualify for clerical work. Yet they found, in the North as in the South, that few white people would hire them as anything but domestic servants or manual laborers.

As African-American neighborhoods in northern cities expanded, some black women found opportunities as teachers there. But the few black-owned businesses large enough to employ clerical workers often hired male office workers, as educated black men found their job options just as tightly restricted. The only place large numbers of black women office workers found employment was Montgomery Ward in Chicago, which employed 1,050 in 1920. Because it was a mail-order business, customers had no direct contact with and never had to know they were served by black clerical workers.

In the 1920s, large numbers of Puerto Ricans also came to the urban North seeking economic opportunity. By 1930, there were 50,000 Puerto Ricans on the mainland, 81 percent of whom lived in New York City. Almost half were women. The Puerto Rican women, like African-American women, found their opportunities

Southern blacks prepare to make the journey north, where they hoped to find more opportunities. Many black women discovered, however, that the jobs open to them were still primarily domestic service and manual labor.

Some black women were able to find jobs as teachers in African-American neighborhoods. Here, students eat lunch in a sparsely furnished Kansas schoolroom.

curtailed. Honorina Irizarry left her job as a secretary in Puerto Rico to join her brother in Brooklyn, New York, where she became a bilingual secretary and a Democratic activist. But she was exceptional. In 1925, only 3.4 percent of all Puerto Rican women in New York, and about 15 percent of the women who worked outside the home, held clerical positions. Language formed one barrier, but race also played a part. Even for assembly line work, one migrant recalled, "If you looked Irish or German, . . . it didn't matter how limited your English was."

Most Puerto Rican women worked in garment or cigar-making sweatshops or in laundries. They usually lived near their work on Manhattan's Lower East Side or in Brooklyn, where they shared rooms with cousins, grandparents, and people from their hometowns.

Despite the tendency to redefine jobs women entered into "women's work," and despite the prevalent racism, women of all races and ethnic groups did make some headway in the professions in the 1920s. Although the percentage of women workers in the professions grew only from 11.9 percent to 14.2 percent, that rise represented an increase of 50 percent in the number of women professionals. By far, most of these professionals were teachers; the next largest number were nurses, but there were also others, such as lawyers, social workers, engineers, and professors. Only the percentage of medical doctors who were female fell, as medical schools imposed a quota on women of no more than 5 percent of a class from 1925 to 1945, and few hospitals accepted female interns.

Professional women came largely from the ranks of college graduates. Both women and men had flooded into colleges after World War I, but women grew as a proportion of the student body until more than 40 percent of college students were women in the 1920s. College students were still the privileged few, however. The proportion of college-age women in the United States who entered college rose from 3.8 percent in 1910 to 7.6 percent in 1920 but would increase to only 10.5 percent by 1930.

Not all college-age women had an equal chance of entering college, even if they could afford it. Many colleges carefully controlled the number of Jewish students on campus, and only at Oberlin did black students constitute even 4 percent of the student body. Black women found black colleges more receptive. By 1929, women formed the majority at some coeducational black colleges. Catholic women also found their options enlarged by special schools. The number of Catholic women's colleges rose from 14 in 1915 to 37 in 1925.

Some college graduates floundered about a bit after graduation, unsure of what they wanted to do. Amelia Earhart, who would become the first woman to fly across the Atlantic alone, at first thought she wanted a career in photography, or maybe social work. An employment agency placed her as a social worker in a poor neighborhood in Boston. There she worked with small children and was remembered chiefly for her large yellow car.

Other women, such as Carrie E. Bullock, had a more focused career path. Bullock was born in Laurens, South Carolina. Her grandparents, who were former slaves, reared her. After she graduated from Scotia Seminary in 1904, she taught school in rural South Carolina, then began her nursing education in 1906. In 1909 she joined the staff of the Chicago Visiting Nurses Association and in 1919 was promoted to supervisor of black nurses. In 1927 she became president of the National Association of Colored Graduate Nurses.

Bullock worked hard to foster communication among black nurses and to increase their opportunities for postgraduate training. By the mid-1920s, there were 2,500 black graduate nurses, but they still

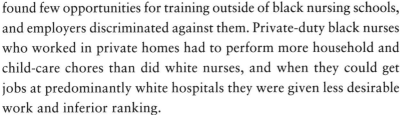

Black nursing students take a class in "drugs and solutions," and a midwife cares for a patient. Black nurses encountered discrimination in the workplace and often took jobs as private nurses.

found few opportunities for training outside of black nursing schools, and employers discriminated against them. Private-duty black nurses who worked in private homes had to perform more household and child-care chores than did white nurses, and when they could get jobs at predominantly white hospitals they were given less desirable work and inferior ranking.

Many women faced cultural as well as gender and racial battles. After years of schooling in Kansas and Los Angeles, Polingaysi Qoyawayma, a Hopi Indian, returned to her reservation in Arizona in the late 1920s to become a teacher and missionary. These jobs gave her a chance to have what she had always dreamed of building, her own house, but they also brought tensions. Told she could not speak the Hopi language to her Hopi first graders, Qoyawayma decided at least to use Hopi legends to teach them to read. In her autobiography, *No Turning Back,* she confessed that she was not sure the missionaries would like the burrowing owls song, which began, "We are little burrowing owls, children of Germinating God." It was hostility from Hopi parents, however, that caught her by surprise. They complained, "What are you teaching our children? . . . We send them to school to learn the white man's way, not Hopi. They can learn the Hopi way at home."

Many professional and businesswomen faced tensions regarding marriage and career. Sue Shelton White, a lawyer born in 1887,

Sue White, a lawyer and Democratic party politician, felt that marriage often stifled a woman instead of bringing fulfillment.

had led the southern wing of the National Women's Party and was a Democratic party politician. Poverty and discrimination had kept her from getting her law degree until she was 36. Her mother, she wrote for a special series on modern women in the *Nation* in 1926, "drew few distinctions between her boys and girls. I have seen my brothers sweep, wipe dishes, and even cook." When her brothers left home, it was Sue who had to carry the water from the well and cut the kindling. By 1926, however, she considered marriage and a career a difficult combination: "Marriage is too much of a compromise; it lops off a woman's life as an individual. Yet the renunciation too is a lopping off. We choose between the frying-pan and the fire—both very uncomfortable."

More professional women married in the 1920s than ever before, but they were still in the minority. In 1910, only 12.2 percent of professional women were married. In 1920, 19.3 percent were; in 1930, 24.7 percent. Other professional women instead found rewarding lifelong support from women, as did Mary Dewson, who was active in the Democratic party and was appointed to a number of political offices. Dewson's partner, Polly Porter, who called her "Puisye," wrote to her when they were apart during World War I: "Little danger that the Puisye will become unnecessary to me—I should be like a ship without sails and a pilot without a north star were she not part of my life."

Yet some professionals, such as psychologist Phyllis Blanchard, did find satisfying marriages. Blanchard earned her doctorate from Clark University, where she met a graduate student in chemistry, Walter Lucasse. When the couple married in 1925, Blanchard kept her own name and continued her career as a child guidance counselor. "He respects my work as much as I do his," she told the *Nation*'s readers. "If he does not feel quite so keenly as I the need of economic independence after marriage, he is more eager that I have leisure for creative work than I am myself."

Blanchard was typical of the new generation of women professionals. In the 1920s, most were not active in social reform, which had gone from being a task of amateur middle-class women to a new profession, social work, that had its own college courses and degrees. Many professional women still wanted to increase women's economic status, improve women's sense of their own worth, reorient family life, and redefine sex roles, but they did so only as individuals.

Although clerical workers and businesswomen were newly conspicuous among women workers in the 1920s, most women workers remained in the occupations that they had in previous decades: domestic service, agricultural labor, and certain manufacturing jobs. For a small subset of the middle and upper classes, work could be seen as inherently satisfying and liberating. For most working women, however, wage labor was a matter of necessity. In the 1920s, despite its reputation as an era of prosperity, 71 percent of U.S. workers earned less than the wage required to support what the government defined as the minimum acceptable standard of living for their families. As a result, in low-income families, 25 percent of all married women worked for wages.

In 1920, five times more married black women than women of any other racial or ethnic group worked outside the home. More than 50 percent of adult black women earned wages. In rural areas most performed back-breaking labor in the fields. In the cities most performed domestic service or laundering. Only 5.5 percent were able to gain employment in manufacturing, a better-paid sector, by 1930.

As the total number of servants declined, black women became a larger and larger share of those remaining. Between one-fifth and one-half of the domestics in New York, Chicago, Philadelphia, and other cities were black women. Almost two-thirds of all gainfully employed black women in the North worked as servants or laundresses. In Pittsburgh, for example, 90 percent of black women earned their way as day workers, washerwomen, or live-in servants.

In service, as in other areas of black life, the growth of black enclaves in the North and the greater degree of freedom there than in the South encouraged a new generation of black female northerners to be more assertive in their relations with whites, to join civil rights groups, such as the National Association for the Advancement of Colored People, and to make their relations with their employers more professional. But by the end of the decade, black women still earned only 20 cents, and white women 61 cents, for every dollar that white men earned.

Mary Dewson (top) was a professional politician who chose partnership with another woman instead of marriage to a man. Psychologist Phyllis Blanchard (bottom) chose a traditional marriage but refused to sacrifice her career.

In the 1920s, most black working women found that whites would hire them only as domestic servants. To break out of this pattern, many in the North struggled to find some sort of work they could do in their own homes.

Domestic service meant something different for the 1,400 Japanese immigrant women who worked in such positions during the 1920s, making up slightly more than one-fourth of the gainfully employed among them. As with black women and other domestic servants, Japanese women found that sometimes employers became like additional family members, visiting them when they were sick, teaching them English, and giving them gifts. Others faced employers who spied on them constantly, suspecting them of stealing or laziness. For the Japanese, however, domestic work was something new and seen as strictly temporary. Mrs. Uematsu told an interviewer, "My husband didn't bring in enough money, so I went out to work. I didn't even think twice about it. If I didn't take a job, people would have started to call me 'Madam' [that is, accusing her of thinking she was too much of a lady to work]. . . . It was like a race; we all had to work as hard as possible." Though the husbands of Japanese immigrant women expected them to contribute to the family income, domestic service, unlike helping in the family business or doing farm work with the family, gave these women an independent wage and time away from their families.

For many black women, on the other hand, domestic service was not a new opportunity to work away from the watchful eye of a husband and to earn an independent income. Rather, it was all that had been available to them for generations. It meant stealing time from their own families and giving it to the families of the very people who foreclosed other opportunities. Substantial numbers of black women, particularly recent migrants from the South to the North, took in home work, making artificial flowers or sewing garments, to avoid having to work for other people's families.

In the Southwest, Chicana employment patterns tended to mirror those of black women in the East, except that a larger percentage were employed in industrial work, particularly in food processing and garment making. The situation for them varied more than for black women. In San Antonio, Texas, Mexican women worked in pecan shelling and clothing factories while black women could get only domestic service jobs. In Colorado, however, the situation was virtually reversed.

Chicana migrant farm workers faced broken-down shacks for housing, long hours in the fields, and wages that would not keep the

family warm and fed and the children clothed decently enough to stay in school through the winter. As a result, they tried to earn money in the winter as domestic servants or laundresses if they could not get work in the canneries, which they preferred.

When black and white women, or Anglo and Chicana women, mingled in factories, the outcome was sometimes predictable but sometimes surprising. In the tobacco factories of Durham, North Carolina, the white women workers arrived from a countryside where whites had gone to great lengths to ensure that blacks held only menial jobs. Their own status depended on being different from the black women who worked in the same factory. In an interview, one worker recalled that black women had to "press hard to hold [them-selves] up" against the harassment of white bosses and coworkers, even at the risk of losing a job. "You're over here doing all the nasty dirty work," another recalled of the blacks' assignment, the gritty work of stripping the stems off tobacco leaves. "And over there on the cigarette side . . . The white women over there wear white uni-forms."

On the other hand, in the canneries of southern California some Anglo women and Chicana workers developed friendships at work. "I had a Jewish friend," Maria Rodriguez told an interviewer. "She

In Texas, Chicanas work in a tamale factory. One worker monitors the tamales rolling by (left), while another wraps the dough (top) and two women separate the corn shucks (bottom).

White women do the relatively clean work of rolling cigars in a factory in Virginia.

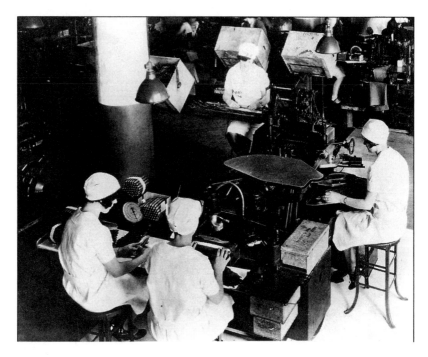

was my work buddy. . . . I never saw her outside the cannery but we were friends at work. . . . We broke the ice by talking about Clark Gable. We were crazy about him. . . . Oh, I loved [the magazine] *True Story,* and she did, too. We'd discuss every little story."

But the 1920s was a hard time to be a factory worker, even without racial tensions. The corporations, courts, and government had taken measures making it harder to strike or to protest conditions. Up to the late 1920s, no union had won a strike in Durham, and few unions were interested in organizing women. In 1920, only 7 percent of women workers were in unions, compared to 25 percent of male workers. Many unions excluded women; others saw them as rivals for work and funds.

Efforts to organize women met with hostility not only from the employers but from male union organizers. Ann Washington Craton, a union organizer herself, reported to the *Nation* in 1927 what happened when one woman organizer got arrested in the course of her job. A small flood of working girls rushed into the union office, demanding that the union pay her bail. But the union men took the news cheerfully. The official in charge told them, "Let her stay in jail. . . . She's all right. Let her stay until we can have a nice, quiet little executive board meeting without her. Then

Black women did the dirty work in the tobacco industry, such as stripping the stems off the tobacco leaves.

we will get her out. Ladies should stay at home. If ladies won't stay at home, let them stay in jail." When Craton and a coworker wanted to organize women in Newark, New Jersey, a union official complained, "Why don't you forget all this business and leave the labor movement to men? It's too rough for women. Why don't you get married?" Craton and her colleague responded, "Perhaps we are married. . . . We still want to organize women into trade unions in Newark."

Despite all the difficulties, there were strikes of women workers in the 1920s, emerging from the desperation of white as well as black women. In March 1929, the women in the inspection room of an Elizabethton, North Carolina, textile mill walked off the job. All but 17 of the 360 walked out, and the next morning they gathered at the factory gate. When the plant manager did not arrive to negotiate, they rushed through the plant and persuaded their coworkers, women and men, to join them.

The young women of Elizabethton wanted more from life than an endless round of low pay; they wanted more than their mothers had. On the picket lines they were feisty, bold, assertive, saucy, firm, and, above all, funny. Trixie Perry and Texas Bill were ringleaders and friends on the picket line. Both women were brought

This letter from the National Textile Workers Union to the editor of the Gastonia Gazette *in North Carolina demonstrates these women's determination to demand their rights as workers.*

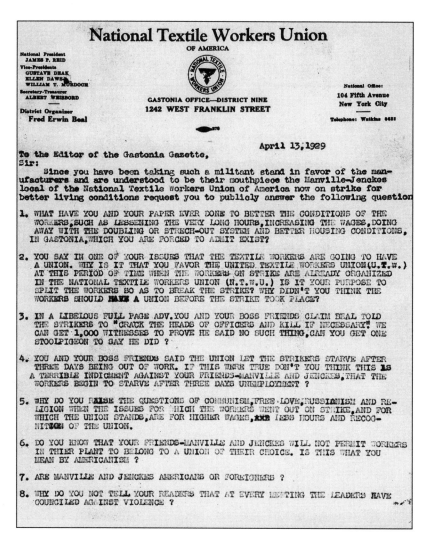

National Textile Workers Union
OF AMERICA

National President
JAMES F. REID

Vice-Presidents
**GUSTAVE DEAK
ELLEN DAWS
WILLIAM T. MURDOCH**

Secretary-Treasurer
ALBERT WEISBORD

District Organizer
Fred Erwin Beal

**GASTONIA OFFICE—DISTRICT NINE
1242 WEST FRANKLIN STREET**

National Office:
**104 Fifth Avenue
New York City**

Telephone: Watkins 6651

April 13, 1929

To the Editor of the Gastonia Gazette,
Sir:

Since you have been taking such a militant stand in favor of the manufacturers and are understood to be their mouthpiece the Manville-Jenckes local of the National Textile Workers Union of America now on strike for better living conditions request you to publicly answer the following question

1. WHAT HAVE YOU AND YOUR PAPER EVER DONE TO BETTER THE CONDITIONS OF THE WORKERS, SUCH AS LESSENING THE VERY LONG HOURS, INCREASING THE WAGES, DOING AWAY WITH THE DOUBLING OR STRECH-OUT SYSTEM AND BETTER HOUSING CONDITIONS, IN GASTONIA, WHICH YOU ARE FORCED TO ADMIT EXIST?

2. YOU SAY IN ONE OF YOUR ISSUES THAT THE TEXTILE WORKERS ARE GOING TO HAVE A UNION. WHY IS IT THAT YOU FAVOR THE UNITED TEXTILE WORKERS UNION (U.T.W.) AT THIS PERIOD OF TIME WHEN THE WORKERS ON STRIKE ARE ALREADY ORGANIZED IN THE NATIONAL TEXTILE WORKERS UNION (N.T.W.U.) IS IT YOUR PURPOSE TO SPLIT THE WORKERS SO AS TO BREAK THE STRIKE? WHY DIDN'T YOU THINK THE WORKERS SHOULD HAVE A UNION BEFORE THE STRIKE TOOK PLACE?

3. IN A LIBELOUS FULL PAGE ADV. YOU AND YOUR BOSS FRIENDS CLAIM BEAL TOLD THE STRIKERS TO "CRACK THE HEADS OF OFFICERS AND KILL IF NECESSARY". WE CAN GET 1,000 WITNESSES TO PROVE HE SAID NO SUCH THING, CAN YOU GET ONE STOOLPIGEON TO SAY HE DID ?

4. YOU AND YOUR BOSS FRIENDS SAID THE UNION LET THE STRIKERS STARVE AFTER THREE DAYS BEING OUT OF WORK. IF THIS WERE TRUE DON'T YOU THINK THIS IS A TERRIBLE INDICMENT AGAINST YOUR FRIENDS-MANVILLE AND JENCKES, THAT THE WORKERS BEGIN TO STARVE AFTER THREE DAYS UNEMPLOYMENT ?

5. WHY DO YOU RAISE THE QUESTIONS OF COMMUNISM, FREE LOVE, RUSSIANISM AND RELIGION WHEN THE ISSUES FOR WHICH THE WORKERS WENT OUT ON STRIKE, AND FOR WHICH THE UNION STANDS, ARE FOR HIGHER WAGES, AND LESS HOURS AND RECOGNITION OF THE UNION.

6. DO YOU KNOW THAT YOUR FRIENDS-MANVILLE AND JENCKES WILL NOT PERMIT WORKERS IN THIER PLANT TO BELONG TO A UNION OF THEIR CHOICE. IS THIS WHAT YOU MEAN BY AMERICANISM ?

7. ARE MANVILLE AND JENCKES AMERICANS OR FOREIGNERS ?

8. WHY DO YOU NOT TELL YOUR READERS THAT AT EVERY MEETING THE LEADERS HAVE COUNCILED AGAINST VIOLENCE ?

to court when they were accused of taunting the National Guard and blocking the way to the mills for new, replacement workers. Women had marched in front of the National Guard draped in the American flag, forcing the guardsmen to present arms each time they passed.

In court, Trixie Perry wore a cap made out of the U.S. flag. When the prosecuting attorney questioned her, she replied, "I was born under it, guess I have a right." When asked if she had blocked the road, she retorted, "A little thing like me block a big road?" Texas Bill was equally unshakable. Asked what she was doing on the road in the early morning, she responded with great dignity, "I take a walk every morning before breakfast for my health." The

guards had threatened the picketing women with guns, used tear gas on them, and arrested them, and the women answered them with laughter.

Like the new generation of black domestic workers and the frustrated union organizers, Trixie Perry and Texas Bill represented a new, more aggressive woman worker. They wanted part of what the 1920s had to offer—not just movies and fine clothes, but independence and the wherewithal to buy those goods for themselves.

Textile workers in Gastonia, North Carolina, walked off their jobs in order to demand better conditions. They were protesting unsanitary conditions, long hours, and low wages.

CHAPTER 4

FUN, FADS, AND THE FAMILY

I t wasn't just the Trixie Perrys in North Carolina or the cannery workers in California who wanted more from life and dreamed of movie stars. In remote Hispanic New Mexican villages, young women had abandoned their sandals and shawls for high heels and elaborate hats. They learned the new, fast, provocative dance steps of the shimmy and the Charleston, and in villages where there were cars, they even went on dates. Before World War I, flappers had started to appear in certain city neighborhoods; now they were everywhere.

Flappers were women who lived—and lived it up—in public. They wore short skirts that exposed their legs and made them freer than prewar styles had allowed. They bobbed their hair, shearing off the long Victorian tresses that had distinguished them from men and taken so much time to maintain. They wore makeup and flesh-colored stockings. It was still close enough to a time when "painted women" had been actresses and harlots to make wearing makeup seem daring, sexually aware, and definitely modern. These women even smoked in public. In recognition of the new womanhood, in 1925 Bryn Mawr College for women lifted its ban on smoking.

Not everyone agreed on the new rules for America's young women, however. In the same year as Bryn Mawr's change in policy, another women's college, Vassar, instituted a ban on smoking, and the University of California at Berkeley did likewise the next year. The edi-

A short-skirted flapper, her necklace flying and her stocking-tops showing, dances the Charleston with abandon on the cover of Life *magazine for February 18, 1926.*

tor of the *Daily Illini,* the student paper of the University of Illinois, called the shimmy "that insult to our whole moral code." But these critics were waging a losing battle. Young women and men were redefining what was proper and seemed to assume that the older systems of order, control, and communication had been destroyed by the war.

Young working women modeled their behavior and their dreams on the movies. In the 1920s, polls showed that movie stars had replaced political, business, and artistic leaders as role models for young people. Ironically, the movies had in turn picked up their themes from the lives of the young working women who made up a large proportion of their audience and had simply glamorized them. The film stories were often created by such women writers as Anita Loos, who wrote *Gentlemen Prefer Blondes* (1925). Fan magazines let their readers know that stars had come from their own ranks: Joan Crawford began as a shop girl in Kansas City, Janet Gaynor as a clerk in a shoe store, and Frances Marion as a stenographer.

Like the lounge at the telephone company, the new picture palaces gave working women a few hours in opulence. In that luxurious atmosphere they watched films like *Ankles Preferred* (1926), in which a bored Madge Bellamy waited on customers in a department store. In *Soft Living* (1928), secretaries labored over long columns of numbers. It was not the life of the working girl that the movies glamorized; it was the chance for escape.

In *Soft Living,* Bellamy portrays a secretary for a divorce lawyer; she hunts for a millionaire and lands one. Office workers and department store clerks, the films showed, worked amid wealthier male bosses and customers. Through spunk and cleverness, according to the movies, they could use their positions to escape the boring monotony of their work.

Young working women did not all rely on marriage as an escape, however. In *Ankles Preferred,* Bellamy becomes successful in the retail trade in her own right and rejects her wealthy suitors, who are interested only in her body. Instead she turns to a trustworthy young man from a lower-class boardinghouse. But the themes of the two films were the same; they echoed the enormously popular novels that Horatio Alger had written 50 years earlier about poor young

Young women in the 1920s helped to redefine what was considered acceptable behavior. Wearing bobbed hair and smoking in public, for example, became fashionable.

men who, through luck, pluck, and virtue, became rich. Usually, their success was assured in part by marrying the boss's daughter. In the 1920s, it was working women who embodied this spirit of entrepreneurial drive. But instead of being the passive maidens rescued by Alger's heroes, now they were in charge of their own futures. Success for them meant marrying the boss, not the boss's daughter.

Reassuringly, the movies tended to end with marriage. Many Americans had begun to fear that the family was being destroyed. If women were free to vote and to live in apartments on their own, and if wives were working outside the home in increasing numbers, then who would keep the home fires burning? The mass media responded by making actual working mothers virtually invisible. Instead, at the same time as the flapper flounced into view, a new glorification of motherhood and marriage emerged. It seemed that after a period of youthful independence and indiscretion, women were to go back home.

It would, however, be a different home, one with fewer children and more machines. A 1927 advertisement in *The New Yorker* showed a middle-class woman sitting in her home reading. The caption asked, "Is this moral reading?" In the background, little stick-figure genies cleaned the house. "The lady appears at ease," commented the ad. "She is. She looks as if running a household worried her not. It

In this cartoon, male office workers joke that the boss has a female secretary. In the 19th century, secretarial jobs were dominated by men.

doesn't. Because at Lewis & Conger she invested in household aids to ease her work, and make it do itself." While the house was cleaning itself, the woman could participate in a fuller life: "So now the lady has time to chortle over The New Yorker to take a hand at running the country, and to think up a discreetly daring new hair cut for herself."

Manufacturers found housewives eager for new household technology. With immigration on the decline in the 1920s, fewer white women were available for domestic service. The black, Asian, and Mexican women who took their places did not quite fill the gap. They, too, wanted their independence. They were less willing to be full-time help and live in the homes of their employers. They preferred day work. In response, fewer homes had servants' quarters, and more women became their own maids.

Many of these women worked for wages outside the home as well as doing housewifery within it. Working-class and middle-class women justified going out to work in terms of their families' needs. Their work tended to be intermittent. It most often hinged on their husbands becoming unemployed, a frequent occurrence in the 1920s. Others worked themselves, rather than withdrawing their children from school to work. "It takes the work of two to keep a family these days," claimed one Muncie, Indiana, woman in *Middletown*, Robert and Helen Lynd's pioneering 1929 study of a "typical" American town. Whereas in earlier decades the two workers would have been a father and a child, it would now be a husband and a wife, because more jobs required a high school education.

For many of the families the Lynds interviewed, however, family needs now meant more than just putting food on the table. "An electric washing machine, electric iron, and vacuum sweeper" also had become necessities for working mothers. "I don't even have to ask my husband any more," revealed another Muncie wife, "because I buy these things with my own money. I bought an ice box last year.... We own a $1,200 Studebaker [car] with a nice California top, semi-enclosed.... The two boys want to go to college, and I want them to. I graduated from high school myself, but I feel if I can't give my boys a little more all my work will have been useless." To many women, being a good mother increasingly meant earning an income to provide purchasing power for the family.

What do the neighbors think of *her* children?

To every mother her own are the ideal children. But what do the neighbors think? Do *they* smile at happy, grimy faces acquired in wholesome play? For people have a way of associating unclean clothes and faces with other questionable characteristics.

Fortunately, however, there's soap and water.

"Bright, shining faces" and freshly laundered clothes seem to make children welcome anywhere . . . and, in addition, to speak volumes concerning their *parents'* personal habits as well.

There's CHARACTER — in SOAP & WATER

PUBLISHED BY THE ASSOCIATION OF AMERICAN SOAP AND GLYCERINE PRODUCERS, INC., TO AID THE WORK OF *CLEANLINESS INSTITUTE*

Any woman who sweeps or beats a rug is tiring herself needlessly. A Little Motor can do it for 1¾ cents an hour

You can buy, from any electrical dealer, household helpers having electrical equipment made by the General Electric Company and bearing the G-E monogram.

This monogram is on fans and MAZDA lamps, and on motors that run vacuum cleaners, washing machines, dishwashers, sewing machines, and many other labor savers.

Ask your electrical company or dealer to help you select the labor-saving electric appliance best suited for your home.

GENERAL ELECTRIC

Advertising in the 1920s was often directed at the middle-class wife and mother. The ad at left, from the New York Cleanliness Institute, was published in the 1928 Ladies Home Journal. *It arouses a mother's fears about appearances and encourages her to buy soap. Above, a General Electric ad advises a woman to buy electric "household helpers" so that she does not exhaust herself with everyday chores.*

Yet despite all the new technology, the women surveyed by the Lynds claimed that they spent more, not less, time on housework in the 1920s than before. Indeed, the time had almost doubled, from 44.3 to 87.5 hours a week. Standards, it seemed, had risen. At the very moment technology could have freed women from much household drudgery for more public activities, suddenly their wash had to be whiter than white. Advertisers played on women's guilt to get them to buy and use the new appliances. "What do the neighbors think of *her* children?" read one 1928 detergent's ad copy in the *Ladies' Home Journal.*

Advertising reached new levels of sophistication through the use of psychology, which was just then becoming popular in the United States. Women made most consumer decisions, so advertisers aimed particularly at them. Advertisements gave housework a new, exalted meaning. Suddenly, washing clothes was not simply laundering, as it had always been, but an expression of love. Getting the gray out of a man's collar was not simply an issue of cleanliness; it was saving the American home. Cooking, cleaning, and other housework all fell into the same category. By 1931, *American Home* could declare that "the careful housekeeper ... will know that prime rib roast, like peach ice cream, is a wonderful stimulant to family loyalty."

These advertisements also indicated the increasing degree to which mothering was seen as a full-time job. With more household technology available, women could have found themselves with more time to spend outside the house. Moreover, the birth rate had declined. In 1800, white women had given birth to an average of 7 children each; in 1900, the average was 3.56; and in 1929, it was only 2.4. Women of all groups were having fewer children. Birth control was still controversial, and it was even illegal in many states, but middle-class women were able to get birth control devices from their private physicians, and in large cities some clinics opened to serve working-class women. However, this still left many working-class women without birth control. And even when they could get birth control information, in an era before the Pill had been invented and when diaphragms and even condoms were not always readily available, they often found their husbands uncooperative. Yet, even though they continued to have more children than middle-class women, birth rates among the working class also declined.

No sooner were there fewer children in the home, however, than experts began to agree that mothers should pay more attention to each one. As advertisements for a laundromat in Muncie asked, "Isn't Bobby more important than his clothes?" And one ad selling electricity declared of the "successful mother" that "she puts first things first. She does not give to sweeping the time that belongs to her

THE BIOLOGY OF
CONCEPTION AND
THE MECHANISM OF
CONTRACEPTION
PRODUCED BY THE
MARGARET SANGER
RESEARCH BUREAU

Women attend a lecture about contraception using materials produced by Margaret Sanger, who had tirelessly campaigned for the legalization and dissemination of birth control.

children. . . . The wise woman delegates to electricity all that electricity can do."

Women who were involved in charitable work, social and political service, and even wage work—despite the fact that most working mothers took paying jobs only out of dire need—were attacked as selfish, as taking jobs away from men who needed them to support families, and as undermining the stability of the home. It was argued that having a woman in the home would keep a child off the streets. "I accommodate my entire life to my little girl," one middle-class woman boasted to the Lynds. With these new ideas, it was hard for working women to feel that they were also successful mothers. It was particularly hard when they lived in homes without electricity. Almost half the homes in the country had no electricity in 1925.

These new ideas of what women should be sharpened social divisions in the United States. One indication of these divisions was the rapid development of ethnically and economically homogeneous suburbs in the 1920s.

The new suburbs were linked to choices about technology and policy that affected women's lives and options. New household technology could have been used, for example, to enhance urban apartment life, which had been on the rise in the previous decades. It could have helped create communal day care facilities and laundries

Parents attend an Independence Day celebration at Scarsdale High School in New York. In such suburban communities, life focused on children and schools, and mothers were often discouraged from taking jobs because of the harm it might cause the youngsters.

that would have left women freer for other activities. In their zeal to save the family from absent mothers, however, policy makers focused on the private home. Each family was to have its own home, and each home its own mother taking care of her own children, using her own kitchen and laundry.

Increasingly, such individual homes were in suburbs. From 1920 to 1930 the population of New York City rose 21 percent; in the same period the population of one of its suburbs, Scarsdale, soared 176 percent. In the 19th century, suburbs had provided homes for people of varying incomes. In the 1920s, the allure of suburbs lay in their very sameness. Suburban developers promised buyers spacious houses with children's playrooms and private lawns. They promised to remove and protect women and children from the dirt and tensions of the city.

In some ways, the suburbs also created another social division: masculine cities and feminine suburbs. Men would leave home for work all day, and women would remain home to tend the children. There, in the newly ubiquitous automobiles, women spent their time driving their children from store to store or to school, all of which had been within walking distance in the city.

Scarsdale, New York, had two organizations influential in civic affairs. One admitted only men, the other only women. Members of the Woman's Club found themselves edged out of advising the village board because they lacked technical training. But the women spent more time in the community than the men. Together Scarsdale's women built a sense of community through social affairs, improved themselves through classes (as women's clubs had done since the mid-19th century), and organized services in the community that the men lacked the time to run. By 1929, the Woman's Club had 1,074 members. In February of that year it offered classes in "physical culture," flower arranging, cooking, current events, French language, and pottery. It also sponsored dances and social nights.

The Woman's Club published the local newspaper, the *Scarsdale Inquirer,* which it had bought for a dollar in 1919. It billed itself as "the country's only newspaper completely owned, operated and staffed by women." The *Inquirer* educated readers on local issues and, beginning in 1931, won prizes from the New York Press Association. The Woman's Club also ran a night school, emphasizing English and citizenship classes.

Like other communities of its type, Scarsdale was in fact less homogeneous than it appeared from its tree-lined streets. In 1925, 910 out of 5,099 residents of Scarsdale were live-in servants. They were not the white, Protestant, native-born people of British heritage who made up Scarsdale's homeowners. Instead, nearly two-thirds of the servants were immigrants, from 30 foreign countries. Irish, Germans, and West Indians accounted for most of them, but there were also 15 Japanese, 7 Italians, and 1 Filipino. Of the American-born servants, more than half were black. Three-fourths of all these servants were women.

The housewives of Scarsdale found few servants eager to live in the suburbs. Women domestics were all too aware that a place like Scarsdale lacked supportive communities of their own ethnic groups. Turnover tended to be high, and those who stayed demanded higher wages. White housewives who wanted white servants found the competition particularly acute. The Woman's Club's night school tried to help matters along. It provided space where servants could socialize and classes where they could work toward citizenship, but few servants attended.

The Scarsdale Woman's Club offered a night school for immigrants who worked as servants in the community. Still, these immigrant women preferred not to live in the suburbs where they worked because they lacked supportive ethnic communities.

The Scarsdale night school excluded African Americans entirely. Despite the shortage of white servants and the fact that black servants would generally work for lower wages, employment agencies could not place all their black applicants. The Episcopal church sponsored the St. Mary's Guild for the parish's black women to aid in church mission work and also provided practice space for Scarsdale's contingent of the county's all-black chorus, but the Woman's Club ignored them.

Despite the confining aspects, for women, of marriage and suburbia, most college women surveyed claimed they aspired above all else to the role of wife. The percentage of women who never married had risen throughout the 19th century to a high of 20 percent; now it dropped to 5 percent. The women's average age at marriage also fell.

At the turn of the century, Jane Addams, an unmarried social activist and founder of Hull House, a settlement house in Chicago, had been one of the most famous, admired, and even revered women in America. Addams had enjoyed a succession of intimate, sustaining relationships with other women who shared her work and her life. In the 1920s, however, the model of femininity was not Jane Addams but the Hollywood starlet.

The 1920s saw the popularization of Sigmund Freud's brand of psychology, particularly its emphasis on the pivotal role of sex in mental health and its depiction of women as incomplete and envious of men. Moreover, at the very moment when women no longer seemed to need marriage on economic or political grounds, people began to define "normal" sexuality in new, narrower terms and to give it increased attention. Despite evidence from a 1926 study that more than one-fourth of adult college-educated women had enjoyed intense emotional relations with other women after puberty, including overt sexual practices, women like Addams were no longer seen as powerful and heroic. Because she never married, Addams's behavior was defined instead as unfulfilled and neurotic. In an economy built around gratification rather than thrift, women's activism outside the home was taken as a sign of an unfulfilled life.

Women did not cease, of course, to rely on other women for support and intimacy. As with politics, however, the range of tolerated behavior shrank, and what had been acceptable before the war

"The Proudest Moment of Our Lives Had Come!"

"This was our own home! There were two glistening tears in Mary's eyes, yet a smile was on her lips. I knew what she was thinking.

"Five years before we had started out bravely together! The first month had taught us the old, old lesson that two cannot live as cheaply as one. I had left school in the grades to go to work and my all too thin pay envelope was a weekly reminder of my lack of training. In a year Betty came—three mouths to feed now. Meanwhile living costs were soaring. Only my salary and I were standing still.

"Then one night Mary came to me. 'Jim', she said, 'why don't you go to school again—right here at home? You can put in an hour or two after supper each night while I sew. Learn to do some one thing. You'll make good—I *know* you will.'

are starting every day.

You, too, can have the position you want in the work you like best. You can have a salary that will give your family the kind of a home, the comforts, the little luxuries you would like them to have. Yes, you can! No matter what your age, your occupation, or your means—you can do it!

All we ask is the chance to prove it. That's fair, isn't it? Then mark and mail this coupon. There's no obligation and not a penny of cost. But it may be the most important step you ever took in your life. Cut out and mail the coupon *now*.

In the 1920s, marriage and family were supposed to be the heights of self-realization and accomplishment for women. The message of this advertisement was that buying a home for the family could bring women such satisfaction.

now was questionable. Some young women even feared to share apartments with each other lest they be suspected of homosexuality. And, in the same way that new fears of radicalism split women's political organizations in the 1920s, new fears of homosexuality made it harder for women to form women's groups whose purpose was women's equality and independence.

Women's focus was not supposed to be other women. According to the advertisers and the new psychologists, their emphasis was supposed to be on how to attract men. Women could find fulfillment, the argument went, only through marriage. In the 19th century, marriage was supposed to involve self-denial and self-sacrifice by women. Now, particularly for the highly educated middle class,

Marriage in the 1920s was supposed to be more fun than it had been, and wives were to be playmates for their husbands. In this family snapshot, the younger women (left) wear daring, more athletic costumes and bobbed hair; their mother (right) dons a more modest suit.

it was supposed to provide sexual satisfaction and self realization. Marriage was supposed to be the gateway to a fuller life, not just for women with low-paying, monotonous jobs but also for college-educated women. Sexual fulfillment in marriage, not a career, was depicted as the ultimate fulfillment for women.

Increasingly, businesses used sex and the desire for sexual attraction and passion in their advertisements. It was women's appearance rather than women's virtue that would secure their husbands' fidelity. Cosmetic companies began to sponsor the first beauty contests. "The first duty of woman is to attract," ran one advertisement. Women had been liberated from the corset only to be entrapped by breast binders, dieting, and makeup. Women were told that by purchasing the right goods they could create the proper effect. "Your masterpiece—yourself," another advertisement promised its readers.

Men as well as women were affected by these trends. Advertisers insisted that the proper collar and the right deodorant would gain a man the desired job. But while men were to use goods to re-create themselves in order to gain jobs, promotions, and public esteem, women were to use goods to re-create themselves in order to get men.

It was in part this focus on sexuality that increased the pressure to legalize birth control. For many people, sex was no longer simply about creating children. With the popularization of psychology, it was about necessary release and pleasure and self-determination. The original birth control activists had aimed to put control of reproduction into the hands of those who had to bear the children—women. By the 1920s, however, the movement had attracted strange bedfellows. Doctors who wanted to legalize it tended to want to control it themselves. Other activists, many of them racist, favored it to keep the "unfit" from reproducing. On the other side, William Henry Cardinal O'Connell of the Catholic church in Boston called a bill to legalize birth control a "direct threat . . . towards increasing impurity and unchastity not only in our married life but . . . among our unmarried people."

Yet, as the decade progressed, more and more birth control clinics opened. In Chicago a judge ruled in 1924 that the health commissioner could not deny a license to a clinic, because to do so amounted to enforcing religious doctrines, which was an illegal joining of church and state. In 1929, when Margaret Sanger's New York City birth control clinic was raided by the police for illegally dispensing birth control devices, the case was thrown out of court. The plainclothes policewoman who had first entrapped the clinic returned later, in her off-duty hours, to seek treatment. Middle-class women could continue to get birth control devices from their private physicians, but only the clinics gave the poor access to contraceptives. By 1930, 55 birth control clinics served the public in 23 cities in 12 states.

Despite the increasing availability of birth control, a new focus on sexuality, and a redefined concept of housework, marriage had a hard time living up to its reputation. Not all women found marriage a way to a fuller life. Tensions arose around consumption. Raising children became more and more expensive, and working-class women

Margaret Sanger (second from left) and her friends wait outside the New York courthouse in 1929. Police raided her clinic in New York City for dispensing birth control devices, but the case was thrown out of court.

The Institute to Coordinate Women's Interests operated this nursery school in 1927. It also founded cooperative laundries and kitchens to help professional women with their household chores.

continued to have less access to money and birth control. Fears of conceiving another child they could ill afford affected these women's sexual pleasure. And expectations of a way of life that did not materialize led to disappointment. In a 1920s study of Muncie, Indiana, when working-class women were asked what gave them the courage to go on in life when they had become thoroughly discouraged, not one of the women mentioned her husband. In difficult times, husbands became not so much individuals as the focus of their wives' problems and fears about jobs and conception.

The divorce rate rose steeply. From 1870 to 1920, the number of divorces in the United States increased by a factor of 15. In 1924, one marriage in seven ended in divorce. More wives than ever before had done paid work during marriage. They knew they had options other than staying in an unsatisfactory marriage. Life was not easy for divorced women, but no longer was divorce the disgrace it had been in the previous century.

All these divorces prompted attacks on women's education, particularly colleges, for not preparing women for their proper vocation: motherhood and wifehood. A few rebels replied by creating institutes like the one Ethel Howe headed at Smith College, the Institute to Coordinate Women's Interests. It aimed to enable college-educated wives to have professional careers by helping to found cooperative nurseries, laundries, shopping groups, and kitchens. Most women's colleges, however, seemed eager to offer some sop to their critics. In 1924, Vassar's board of trustees created a whole interdisciplinary school of "Euthenics," which focused on the development and care of the family, including such courses as "Husband and Wife," "Motherhood," and "The Family as an Economic Unit." At the University of Chicago, Dean of Women Marion Talbot pioneered a graduate program in home economics.

The trajectory from flappers to home economics epitomized an essential dilemma for women's roles in the 1920s. If women could support themselves and represent themselves politically, why should they bother getting married? In the 1920s, prompted by the mass media and advertising, the family had had to change its meaning. No longer would it be portrayed as a necessary economic unit, though it often still was, or as a microcosm of the social and political structure. Now family was about self-fulfillment, consumption, and nur-

A special issue of Survey *magazine in 1926 offers a variety of articles about "woman's place" in society and the home.*

turing the newly discovered psyche of the child. Writing on women and the state in the mid-1920s, journalist Suzanne LaFollette saw marriage as an economic trap that stifled the independence of both men and women. But marriage did not end in the 1920s. Individual "new women" might get divorced, but marriage as an institution changed its rationale and endured.

CHAPTER 5

REBELS

While her husband went to Europe in 1925, anthropologist Margaret Mead set off for Samoa. There she studied adolescent girls. When she published her results, in *Coming of Age in Samoa* (1928), she had a best-seller. In her autobiography, she offered this advice: "Women must learn to give up pandering to male sensitivities, something at which they succeeded so well as long as it was a woman's primary role, as a wife, to keep her family intact, or, as a mistress, to comfort her lover." Modern women, Mead implied, had a larger role, and men would have to look after their own sensitivities.

Mead was not alone in her rebellion against the 1920s formula of men-centered women. Frances Perkins kept her own name when she got married in her 30s, in the midst of a career in social welfare. She irritably wrote the Mount Holyoke College alumnae office, "I ... think that some meddlesome person has told you to change my name on your records. I do not use my husband's name either socially or professionally and it makes a great deal of trouble and annoyance to have my mail so addressed, as it in that case does not reach me directly."

When New York lawyer Crystal Eastman and her husband had to move out of their apartment because the building was to be torn down, they moved into two separate places instead of one. It was Eastman's idea. "You're breaking up our home," her husband had said. But according to an article she wrote for *Cosmopolitan* in 1923,

Anthropologist Margaret Mead wears traditional Samoan dress while doing research on Tau Island. Mead was one of many modern women who stressed that women should not be dependent on men.

Tennis champion Helen Wills rebelled against the idea that women were dainty and delicate. As an athlete, she presented a strong and vigorous image.

she had replied staunchly, "No I'm not. I'm trying to hold it together." She took a small apartment for herself and her children, and her husband moved to a rooming house near his office. "Every morning," she told her readers, "like lovers, we telephone to exchange the day's greetings and make plans for the evenings. . . . It is wonderful sometimes to be alone in the night and just know that someone loves you. In other moods you must have that lover in your arms. Marriage under two roofs makes room for moods." In a decade when the country had decided that marriage was about sex and romance but that life was about the struggle for individuality, Eastman's solution seemed fitting, if unorthodox.

Other rebellions also took into account 1920s sensibilities and options. Tennis champion Helen Wills personified vigorous, rather than delicate, womanliness. Wills at least had the support of her family in shaping her career. Her father, a physician, had taught her all he knew of tennis, and when she could beat him he set her up with coaches who helped her, at age 17, win the 1923 National Women's Championship. Zelda Fitzgerald, on the other hand, was a southern belle, trained to be beautiful, decorative, and amusing. Her husband, the novelist F. Scott Fitzgerald, expected a companionate marriage. He wanted her to amuse herself quietly when he worked and to play when he played. Her sense of emptiness in this life, however, led her into an affair and then to ballet and writing. Even though he wrote novels that chronicled the new morals of the 1920s, her husband objected to her writing in traditional terms: "I am the highest paid short story writer in the world. . . . That is all my material. None of it is your material. . . . I would like you to think of my interests. That is your primary concern, because I am the one to steer the course, the pilot. . . . I want you to stop writing fiction."

Many women did not stop writing fiction in the 1920s, no matter who told them to, and many of those writing were black women who joined Harlem's literary circles. Harlem had only recently ceased to be a Jewish immigrant enclave and to become a large black community within New York City. For both blacks and whites it stood as a symbol of African-American aspirations and possibilities. It was the one place an African American could be anything.

College-educated black men and women flocked to Harlem from all over the nation. Most other towns had room for perhaps one black doctor or lawyer, who would then serve primarily—and sometimes only—the black community. In Harlem, the largest black community in the country, blacks owned businesses and real estate, were librarians and teachers, and ran literary magazines and cultural gatherings.

In the Harlem of the 1920s, the women and men writers of what became known as the Harlem Renaissance—because of the flowering there of black self-expression—also worked to create a new image of blackness. They were a varied lot. Louise Thompson's family had moved to the Far West as domestic help. She grew up in Oregon and California with few other blacks, and often was taken for white or, sometimes, Mexican. When "passing" for white she could not recognize her black friends in public. She began to long for a stronger race identity.

While Thompson was studying at the University of California, she heard W.E.B. Du Bois speak. He was a black equal rights activist and scholar who had been instrumental in founding the National Association for the Advancement of Colored People (NAACP). It

F. Scott and Zelda Fitzgerald on their honeymoon. Fitzgerald incorporated many of his wife's traits into his female characters and used events from their life in his fiction. He did not want her to use this material for her own novels, however.

Black intellectuals and artists often met in the Dark Tower, a salon in Harlem. Poems by Langston Hughes and Countee Cullen were painted on the walls.

was the first time she had seen a black man appear in public without self-effacement. After earning a degree in business administration, Thompson taught at Hampton Institute, a black college in Virginia founded by white philanthropists after the Civil War. There she supported a student strike against what they saw as paternalism in the school, a condescending and parental-like control by the administration. She then headed for Harlem.

Regina Andrews, by contrast, came from a wealthier background. Her father was a lawyer in Chicago, and she became a librarian in Harlem. She made her apartment a meeting place for the literary and artistic set.

Another Harlem writer, Jessie Fauset, came from an old Philadelphia family and graduated Phi Beta Kappa from Cornell. She served as literary editor of *The Crisis,* the NAACP's journal and the most common outlet for Harlem writers. She also wrote four novels, as well as poems and stories. Fauset's novels portrayed middle-class African Americans in middle-class professions striving for middle-class goals. She emphasized similarities between blacks and whites. In her foreword to *Chinaberry Tree* (1931), she declared that the black man "started out as a slave but he rarely thinks of that. To himself he is a citizen of the United States whose ancestors came over not along with the emigrants in the *Mayflower,* it is true, but merely a little earlier in the good year, 1619. . . . And he has a wholesome respect for family and education and labor and the fruits of labor." Although Fauset criticized white society in her novels, she refused to go beyond a mild rebuke.

Others took the rebellion further. Harlem was no paradise. The death rate for blacks in New York City was almost twice that for whites; 60 percent of the black working women in New York City worked as laundresses or servants. Although blacks in New York appeared in 316 of the 321 possible occupations in the 1920 census, they could not be served in many of the Harlem theaters where they performed.

Yet some whites flocked from their homes in Manhattan to Harlem's nightlife. Tired of and alienated from the modern industrial world—especially after witnessing the carnage of World War I—some whites were on the prowl for something fresh, for a less complicated existence, more in harmony with nature and each other.

Aided by popularized anthropology and psychology, many whites rebelling against the materialism of the decade looked to the poorer Harlemites for their spiritual salvation. They dipped into Harlem for an evening, making up audiences that, as Walter White, then head of the NAACP, put it, "receive [blacks] as artists but refuse to accept them as men."

The Harlem Renaissance writers, however, had something else in mind. They rejected this white image of blacks as primitive, one-dimensional, and uncomplicated. "For generations in the mind of America," wrote Rhodes scholar and Harvard graduate Alain Locke in his essay "The New Negro," "the Negro has been more of a for-

The cover of The Crisis *for April 1923 was illustrated by Laura Wheeler. As the journal of the NAACP, it was a prime outlet for Harlem Renaissance writers and artists.*

mula than a human being." For poet Langston Hughes, the literary movement was a declaration of independence, a chance for black people to create their own images. In 1926 he wrote, "If white people are pleased we are glad. If they are not, it doesn't matter. We know we are beautiful. And ugly too. . . . If colored people are pleased we are glad. If they are not, their displeasure doesn't matter either. We build our temples for tomorrow, strong as we know how, and we stand on the top of the mountain free from within ourselves."

But reality was more complicated than Hughes's declaration. Writers needed money to survive. For a time, Hughes, Thompson, and Zora Neale Hurston shared the same patron, a wealthy, white Park Avenue matron named Mrs. Rufus Osgood Mason. Hughes and Thompson quickly moved on. Hurston stayed longer. Mason was both generous and controlling. She tried to ensure that her protégées stuck to the image of the simple, emotional primitive. Hurston had to tread a fine line to write what she wanted.

Like Margaret Mead, Hurston had studied anthropology at Columbia University. Unlike Mead, she returned to her own roots, an all-black town in Florida, to collect folklore. Mason funded her. Hurston centered her novels on that world. They were not filled with middle-class blacks striving for acceptance in the white world. Instead they depicted, often in dialect, a black world with little direct interaction between blacks and whites. Her characters filled many Harlem Renaissance writers with dismay. As one critic complained, "Her darkies always smiled through their tears, sang spirituals on the slightest provocation, and performed buck dances when they should have been working."

This criticism missed the essential radical point to her stories, which were radical both in their blackness and in their feminism. Indeed, that combination may have been one source of her friction with Harlem's black intellectual elite. As Hurston depicted the world, the competition among blacks and black men's subordination of women stemmed from their relations with white society. Her novels showed African Americans left to themselves, in towns like the one in which she had been born, developing an alternative to white society, a communal culture of social equality. If Hurston's characters spoke in dialect, they were not mindless primitives. Her characters

Author Jessie Fauset wrote about middle-class African Americans in her novels and emphasized middle-class goals.

Zora Neale Hurston incorporated the folklore of her native Florida into her novels. Her books described black communities that had little or no interaction with whites.

and their thoughts were complex, but it was not a white world that she described.

Nor was it a man's world. The men in Hurston's stories had a noticeable tendency to die off just before the end. Women, on the other hand, survived. Hurston's struggle, like that of Langston Hughes, was for autonomy. But it seemed that she could not conceive of a way for women to achieve full growth and become fully human without writing off the men who, in her stories, kept trying to define them.

There were other women who also sought refuge and self-definition in Harlem. In the 1920s, Harlem hosted a lesbian subculture.

Popular blues singer Bessie Smith participated in the lesbian subculture that flourished in Harlem in the 1920s.

Lesbian communities also existed in Salt Lake City, Greenwich Village in New York City, San Francisco, and other cities, but Harlem's was the largest.

For the first time, in the 1920s, love between women was assumed to be sexual, even when it was not, and "homosexual" was becoming an identity. At this stage, the popular fascination with Freud had two opposing effects. On the one hand, it made people more comfortable with sexual experimentation. In this view, bisexuality became an adventure. On the other hand, popular Freudian psychology defined exclusive homosexuality as a disease. The writer Edna St. Vincent Millay, resisting pressure to add men to the women she loved, referred to Freud's ideas as an "attempt to lock women up in the home and restore them to cooking and baby-tending."

Harlem, a place already identified with primitivism in the minds of many whites, seemed the ideal place to give in to sexual desires. Although blacks in general shared the mixed feelings of whites toward homosexuality, a series of bars catering particularly to homosexuals opened their doors to all comers.

Both white and black women enjoyed the lesbian subculture. Many of the black blues stars participated. Blues had reached its first great popularity in the 1920s, and blues singer Bessie Smith was among the most highly paid women entertainers. She and Ma Rainey, another blues singer, both of whom were married, found a way to keep their lesbian affairs in Harlem from harming their popularity with their audiences. Ma Rainey recorded "Prove It on Me Blues," about a woman who preferred women, but she carefully cultivated an image of herself as being interested in men too. Bisexuality could simply seem twice as sexy.

Concern with individualism and sexuality dominated the decade. Even the rebellions of the 1920s took their shape from those impulses. Nevertheless, the reconciliation was incomplete. The decade had not resolved the dilemma its opening years had raised. With Zora Neale Hurston able to have women achieve fulfillment only by killing off men, with "New Style" feminists thinking they had to be like men, with no legitimacy granted to organized feminism, with no good fit between ideology and reality (seen most clearly in the case of working mothers), women had only a fragile foothold in the

Ma Rainey cultivated an image of bisexuality in Harlem and even recorded a blues song about women who preferred women.

brave new world. They would be ill-equipped, despite having the vote, despite having broken into the human race, to face challenges that the 1930s depression would mount to their right to work outside the home at all.

MAKING DO WITH DISASTER

In the mid-1930s, scholar Margaret Jarman Hagood drove deep into rural North Carolina to talk with more than 250 white farm tenant families for her book *Mothers of the South* (1939). In it she described the life of a typical woman named Mollie, from when she was 10 years old until Hagood met her at age 37. Mollie was pregnant again and wishing, she told Hagood, that "doctors would tell you what to do when they say, 'Now you shouldn't have any more children.'"

As a child, Mollie had stayed home from school on wash days to help her mother scrub her father's and brothers' overalls and the baby's diapers in a huge wash pot on top of a wood fire her brothers kindled before school. She worked in a dress worn and outgrown, saving the year's two new dresses for school and church.

In 1920, when Mollie was 16, she heard about a neighboring girl who had moved to a town to work in a tobacco factory, about the money she made, and the things she could buy. Telling no one, Mollie made a bundle of her clothes and left one morning, early, just as the backbreaking work of picking cotton was about to begin. For four months she boarded with a relative of her father and made $20 a week. She bought a coat for $15, high-top shoes for $11, and a hat for $8 and spent the rest on all the small items denied her on the farm. She reveled in this taste of "urban" culture and the freedom to buy what she chose. She ate store-bought food for the first

A South Carolina farm woman inside her house in 1930. In the rural South, economic depression existed throughout the 1920s.

Rural black families, like this one in Missouri, rarely shared in the prosperity and progress found in the cities.

time and shared meals and good times with the five other women boarding in the same house.

But then her father called her back home and forbade her to return to the factory. She married before the age of 20, and by the time she was 23 she was pregnant for the third time. Her husband, Jim, bought her one Sunday dress each year, when he could afford it. At the time she talked with Hagood, she and Jim lived in a three-room log cabin, and Mollie sold eggs to bring in some extra money. She was determined that her little girl would go to school regularly and get a wage-earning job, far from farming.

Life had changed little for Mollie over 20 years. For many rural women like her, the drastic economic downturn of the Great Depression started long before the stock market crashed in 1929. For tenant farmers in particular, the rural South had experienced hard times ever since the Civil War, and farmers in the rural West had never recovered the prosperity they had enjoyed during World War I. Black families fared particularly badly. In Macon County, Georgia, for example, most black farm families lived in houses with dirt floors. Only one-fifth of these homes had indoor water, and three-fourths had no sewage disposal. Black income in Macon County averaged less than a dollar per day.

Young women like Mollie were part of a family economy in which their labor helped the family survive but gained them no cash. Young men could work for pay in the fields of more prosperous farmers, but if women wanted to earn money—and be able to spend it—they had to head for town. And so they did. Between 1910 and 1930, women in their early 20s migrating to Minneapolis outnumbered men by almost two to one.

However, those hopeful rural migrants who arrived in the cities after 1929 confronted an urban America reeling from an economic collapse that touched every sector of the economy. Factories closed. Businesses failed. When one-fifth of the country's banks failed, 9 million families lost their savings. As many as one-third of all workers were either unemployed or on short hours and reduced wages. In some places and for certain groups, the numbers were even higher. By the end of 1930, 70 percent of the African Americans in Charleston, South Carolina, and 75 percent of those in Memphis, Tennessee, were jobless. So were more than half the black women in Chicago and three-fourths of them in Detroit. Only eight states offered workers any form of unemployment insurance. There was no federal unemployment program. Workers' families lost the furniture and cars they had bought on installment plans because they could not meet the payments. Many also lost their homes. By 1934, in Indianapolis, Indiana, and Birmingham, Alabama, more than half the home owners had defaulted on their loans. So had 40 percent of home owners in 20 other cities.

If the 1920s had been a time of optimism and energy for many people in the United States, the 1930s began with fear and desperation. The basic assumptions of the previous decade—that technology was the answer to all problems, that businessmen knew best how to run the country, and that women's and men's greatest duty to society was to seek their own personal satisfaction—tottered.

As for the new women of the 1920s, what had looked like vigorous independence and strong-mindedness in the flapper now seemed careless, selfish, and superficial. A whole generation found themselves tempted by an older, comforting vision of mom as a plump, slightly frazzled woman who could be relied on to sacrifice herself to nurture others and make it all better. That shift, along with the economic realities of the depression, created a different set of possibilities and limits for women.

Families coped with economic disaster in different ways. Helen Hong Wong had come to the United States in 1928 from Hong Kong dreaming of luxury. Instead she found herself, as she told an interviewer, working "like a slave" in her husband's restaurant and laundry. "I was not prepared for such a hard time," she recalled. "I found no streets paved with gold." Despite all the potatoes she peeled and the vegetables she chopped, the couple lost their restaurant in Fort Wayne, Indiana, during the depression. "People couldn't afford to eat," she concluded. Helen and her husband moved to Chicago but could find no work and could not collect welfare. Finally, her husband went to Chinatown and borrowed money from gamblers.

Other families also relied on ethnic connections. Many Americans were only a generation away, if that, from immigration. They still lived in neighborhoods where the shopkeepers and the customers alike spoke Polish, Italian, Spanish, or Yiddish. In Chicago, Mary Rupcinski and her husband had taken in tenants for years. During the depression, they let them stay on for months, even though the tenants could not pay their rent because they had lost their jobs. Neighborhood grocers often carried people on credit as long as they could, and neighborhood banks sometimes held off foreclosing on homes. Relatives doubled up, moving their families together into a single apartment or house. People shared.

Women often had a strong role in keeping such relationships alive. They visited, watched each other's children, and shared recipes. This all seemed part of their role as sustainers of family welfare, providers of food and clothing. Moreover, women needed such networks because they could not make as much money as men could.

The depression proved the fragility of these networks. Without the rent from their tenants, the Rupcinskis ultimately could not make their mortgage payments, and they lost their house. Neighborhood banks closed. Ethnic organizations went bankrupt. When their neighborhood networks failed, women turned to other avenues for help. They cashed in insurance policies, and they visited welfare agencies.

It was hardest for single women to get food, shelter, work, or money from welfare agencies. Policymakers assumed that these women all had families somewhere that would care for them. In New York City, the $8 million government work-relief program focused on

During the depression, many people depended on help from their ethnic community to survive. This Jewish group in Los Angeles also collected clothes for needy people in their native Russia.

helping male heads of families. It took the private effort of well-known women to raise $350,000 to provide work for what they called the unemployed "army of women clerical workers." Men could sleep in flophouses, places charging 25 cents a night to sleep on a mattress in a large common room, but there were no flophouses for women. In 1930, the mayor of Minneapolis offered them the city jail.

Women continued to come to the city seeking work, but there was little to be had. In January 1930, one agency in Minneapolis could place only 70 of the 300 women who applied. Women factory workers, teachers, and clerical workers who had lost their jobs turned to domestic service. Some women, in desperation, turned to prostitution.

At the unemployment bureaus, women waited for hours, day after day. Many had eaten little for weeks or months. Journalist Meridel Le Sueur wrote of one woman who "went crazy yesterday at the YW[CA]." She had had no work for eight months. As she kept saying, "You've got to give me something," the woman in charge of the agency began scolding the girl for her scuffed shoes. According to Le Sueur, "they were facing each other in a rage both helpless, helpless."

The Great Depression reached into every corner of the country, but it did not affect all people equally. For many middle-class women of all races, the depression required certain changes in spending pat-

Single women who could find no other work to support themselves sometimes turned to prostitution. At left, a St. Louis woman plies her trade; above is the mug shot of a 21-year-old Austrian immigrant arrested in Pittsburgh.

In Employment Agency *(1937), Isaac Soyer depicted the exhaustion that overcame men and women trying to find jobs when they knew that few were available.*

terns: buying cheaper cuts of meat, feeding the homeless men who stopped at the back door, and doing without new clothes. Some of these women continued to do community volunteer work, raising money for the unemployed. They saw the food lines, but they did not have to join them.

Among women workers, race played an important role. The fierce competition for jobs fueled racial resentments. Mexican-American and African-American women were the first to lose their jobs and the last to get relief from welfare agencies. Often, they were already living on the margin of survival. Before 1933, when the Prohibition amendment making the manufacture or sale of alcoholic beverages illegal was repealed, many of these women turned to bootlegging, making their own beer or liquor and selling it.

Other women struggled to survive within the bounds of the law. On street corners in the congested neighborhoods of the Bronx in New York City, black women, old and young, dressed as neatly as they could and stood ready to sell their cleaning services for an hour or two, or even for the whole day, for as little as 15 cents an hour. This arrangement was called the Bronx Slave Market. The two black women who investigated the Market for the NAACP's *Crisis* in 1935 found that these low rates had produced a new set of employers. Women of the lower middle-class who could not have dreamed of affording a servant during the 1920s could afford one now.

The number of married women in the labor force increased by 52 percent during the 1930s. By 1940, although the percentage of single women who worked for wages had dropped slightly, 15.6 percent of married women worked for pay. Most of the increase consisted of white native-born women, who provided only 43 percent of the total female labor force in 1930 but 70 percent in 1940. Of these white working women, the fastest-growing group was that between the ages of 25 and 45, the group most likely to have children at home. Their ability to hire African-American and Mexican-American women for extremely low wages made it easier for them to leave the home.

Not all married women coped with hard times by leaving the home. Many women took in home work. In Durham, North Carolina, women who had worked in tobacco factories now tagged tobacco sacks at home. In Rhode Island, women who had lost their jobs in the textile mill took home worsted wool to mend. Home work networks relied on ethnic neighborhood ties. In West Warwick, Rhode Island, the lace makers for American Textile were Portuguese women; the lace pullers who worked at home for Rhode Island Lace were Italian women; and the lace pullers who worked for Richmond Lace in the rural southwestern part of Rhode Island were descended from English, Scotch, or Irish immigrants. There were advantages to home work for women. It allowed them to tend their own children, gather in chatty groups with other home workers, and barter among themselves, using their receipts for work completed as a kind of currency.

Home work had disadvantages, however. In San Antonio, Texas, the presence of thousands of temporarily unemployed families, largely Mexican-American, attracted home work industries from as far away as New York. Garment makers fleeing New York's higher labor costs joined the local pecan-shelling companies that were providing home work in San Antonio. As in Rhode Island and New York, where Puerto Ricans worked in the garment industry, the sewing required was hand work, in this case including embroidery. As the depression took hold, prices dropped continually. Between 1929 and the mid-1930s, employers cut

Middle-class women had to change their spending habits during the depression but many still found time to do charitable work and deliver food and clothes to the unemployed.

Many farm families fared better than urban families during the depression because they could depend on food from their crops and livestock.

the rates by 50 percent. For Chicanas, as for other home workers, the lack of alternatives kept them on the job. In 1936, the Women's Bureau of the U.S. Department of Labor interviewed home workers in San Antonio and Laredo, Texas. It found that many of the workers lived in one- or two-room shacks without plumbing or electricity. In one home/workshop there was no light source and the renter had to cook all her meals outside. She shared water and toilet facilities with 15 other families.

Moreover, home work encouraged competition among women. In any given city, factory women complained that home workers undercut their wages and their working conditions. And competition between cities also affected women, as garment manufacturers pitted Puerto Rican home workers in the East against Chicanas in the Southwest.

Despite all the rural women fleeing the farms, a Hispanic woman who lived in northern Colorado during the depression told an interviewer, "People on the farm were better off than downtown; we had our gardens." Even relatively prosperous farm women—owners, not tenants—in general produced as much as 70 percent of what their families consumed in clothing, toys, and food. They not only gardened but raised poultry. During the depression, women increased the size of their gardens and the number of their hens. They made more butter from their dairy cows and sold it. They cut up the sacks that held large amounts of flour and sewed them into underwear. In the previous decade, they had proudly begun to participate in a culture of store-bought goods. Now they began to can food again. Government agents dragged huge canning kettles across the mountains of northern New Mexico and eastern Tennessee so that women in remote farming villages could preserve their food.

Even with all this work, rural children suffered from malnutrition, and rural women faced childbirth without a doctor or midwife because they could afford neither the medical fees nor the gasoline for transportation. The women resented their declining standards of living, particularly those from better-off farm families who owned their own farms and had, during the 1920s, aspired to participate in the new domestic technology of indoor bath-rooms, modern stoves and heating, and supercleanliness. One farm wife wrote to the *Dakota*

Farmer's "Home Page" in 1935, "When one has not modern conveniences, one can't keep the house bright; especially when one has no rugs, no paint on the floor, nor anything else of that sort to make things look nice. . . . It is very different in beautiful houses where everything runs with power and everything is up-to-date." Through national women's magazines and the Sears Roebuck catalogs, these women had internalized the 1920s message that women's duty was to create a beautiful home and a beautiful self. Hard outdoor labor no longer seemed suitable to the "modern homemaker." The women writing the advice columns in farm magazines held each other to city standards of tidiness. Women without toilets or sinks, without running water in their homes, who nevertheless preserved 1,500 quarts of food a year, were advised to try wearing powder and rouge to please their husbands.

Rural women canned and preserved fruits and vegetables during the depression, even though many had hoped in the 1920s to start buying some of their food and other goods from stores.

In the 1920s, people had worried about how to keep the family together when faced with women's increasing independence. Now they worried about how to keep men in the family as it became clear that many women still depended on the income of men, after all, and many men were now unemployed. Powder and rouge were not enough. Divorce rates dropped in the 1930s, but more because people could not afford the costs of an official divorce than because families were staying together. Desertion ran rampant. In 1931, an official at the Urban League, an organization to promote the welfare of African Americans, described the difficulties of one Pittsburgh woman. When her husband lost his job at a steel mill, he was told that "he needn't trouble looking for a job as long as there is so many white men out of work." Faced with supporting six children, all under 16 years old, and no way to do so, her husband simply left, convinced that her chances of getting help from welfare agencies would improve if he were not living at home. When the woman applied to the city's welfare office for aid, she complained bitterly, "I guess us colored folks don't get hungry . . . like white folks."

White men left for the same reasons, going out to look for work and never returning, leaving their wives to try to convince increasingly suspicious and underfunded charity agents and city officials that they were virtuous enough to be worthy of aid. Families that stayed together tried not to add new members. The birthrate, which

A field nurse employed by the Negro Project visits a black family to talk to the parents about birth control.

had been declining steadily for a century, hit its lowest point in 1933, when only 75.7 of every 1,000 women of childbearing age gave birth.

In 1936, a federal appeals court overruled an earlier law that had classified birth control information as obscene and thus illegal to dispense. That decision still left state laws intact, however. The number of birth control clinics nationwide rose from 55 in 1930 to 300 by 1938, but in some states and in many rural areas women still had no access to birth control. In 1937, North Carolina became the first state to provide contraceptives with tax dollars, and six others soon followed. Ironically, North Carolina's reasoning was not that birth control was a human right but that birth control would reduce the black population.

Despite statistics showing that black women had fewer babies than white women with similar incomes and living situations, many white southern officials in states with large black populations feared a black population explosion. In 1939, the Birth Control Federation of America responded to eager southern state governments by developing "The Negro Project," a program to disseminate birth control information, which they carefully staffed with local black community leaders.

Whatever the logic, one quarter of all women in the United States in their 20s during the depression never bore children. This was the highest rate of childlessness for any decade. Many people simply decided not to get married, and marriage rates fell.

With men unable to fulfill their traditional roles as providers and many deserting their homes, women were increasingly left to run the family, with little money and few opportunities. Many men and women at all levels of society worried that chaos would follow. To them, orderly society depended on a family organized around a strong, dominant father. A small number of people did suggest that the solution might lie in providing more opportunities for the women left running the family, but most people focused instead on men's unemployment and on how to keep the family together. These people tended to decide that the real culprits were married working women. They saw those women as stealing jobs from married men.

The media, which had made married working women invisible in the 1920s, now often vilified them. During the 1920s, married women had experienced discrimination at the local level, particularly as teachers. By the early 1930s, public officials such as New York Assemblyman Arthur Swartz were calling them "undeserving parasites." Several cities ordered the dismissal of wives whose husbands earned what they defined as "living wages." In 1931, legislators in Massachusetts, New York, and California introduced bills to limit government employment of married women. The federal government's 1932 Economy Act required that when personnel reductions took place in the executive branch, married persons be the first discharged if their spouse also worked for the government. Women earned less than men, even for the same job, so given the choice, a family would logically retain the higher-salaried man's job and let the wife go unemployed.

Many women's groups rallied in opposition to this legislation. The leaders of the Business and Professional Women's Clubs declared in their journal, *Independent Woman,* "Such legislation is not only a blow to married women, but through implication to all women workers and to marriage itself." Women in government work had to choose between a job and a husband.

Despite mounting protests, the controversial clause of the Economy Act was not repealed until 1937. In 1936, George Gallup, witnessing the results of his new public opinion polls, in which 82 percent of the respondents agreed that wives should not work if their husbands were employed, observed that he had "discovered an issue on which voters are about as solidly united as on any subject imaginable—including sin and hay fever."

Local governments followed the lead of the federal government. Despite the fact that during the 1920s 60 percent of towns and cities

Volunteers in the 1930s selling the Birth Control Review. *In 1936, the federal courts overturned a law that declared birth control information obscene.*

would not hire married teachers and 50 percent forced a teacher who married to retire, the proportion of female teachers who were married almost doubled during that decade, reaching more than 150,000 by 1930. In many states, rural areas were particularly likely to hire or retain married women. The depression saw communities cut back on school funds, reduce the number of teachers, and slash their salaries. Amidst all this, they also reduced the number of married teachers. By 1940, only 13 percent of communities would hire wives as teachers, and only 30 percent would retain women teachers who got married. The percentage of male teachers rose from 19 percent to 24.3 percent of teachers during the 1930s. Married women teachers, however, did not disappear. Indeed, over the same period they increased from 17.9 percent to 22 percent of all female teachers, but the absolute number of women teachers had dropped by 81,000.

Many communities in the 1930s would not hire married women as teachers so that unemployed men and single women could take these jobs.

On the other hand, women retained their hold on clerical positions, which steadily increased in number in the 1930s. Advocates of women's employment found themselves making a virtue out of the fact that women were by and large limited to certain jobs. The number of women in male-dominated professions, including science and college teaching, decreased in the 1930s. Because all women's jobs were threatened, women who were trying to salvage these jobs reinforced the notion that some occupations were particularly suited to women. Running beauty salons, of which there were 40,000 by 1930, or working as dental hygienists and occupational therapists all offered women increased opportunities. Such jobs had the added advantage of placing women where they would not compete with men. The proportion of women working outside the home rose only slightly from 1930 to 1940, from 24.4 percent to 25.4 percent, a far smaller rise than in previous decades.

In the mass media women seemed to be receiving mixed messages. On the one hand, in 1930, the *Ladies' Home Journal* featured a former career woman confessing, "I know now without any hesitation . . . that [my husband's job] must come first." In 1931, the popular magazine *Outlook and Independent* quoted the dean of Barnard College, a women's college in New York City, telling her students that "perhaps the greatest service that you can render to the community . . . is to have the courage to refuse to work for gain." And on its front page in 1935, the *New York Times* reported that women "suffering from masculine psychological states" and an "aversion to marriage" were being "cured" by the removal of their adrenal gland.

In this atmosphere, not only were women workers under fire, but women who centered their lives on women rather than on men came under attack. Lesbianism was no longer chic. Lesbian bars almost disappeared. Homosexuality was now seen by many people as just one more threat to the family.

On the other hand, movie houses showed zany screwball comedies with more complicated lessons. Often, deliciously ditsy, incompetent women were rescued by sensible, capable men. Yet the men in these movies were also frequently portrayed as bumbling or slower-witted than the women. Sometimes the men were people who needed joy and whimsy restored to their lives, not

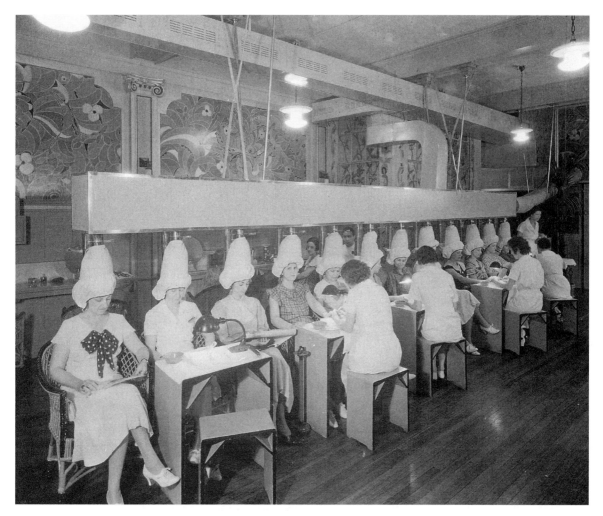

an unexpected theme for a nation in the throes of an economic depression.

In other movies, however, women were by no means incompetent. The women portrayed by Katharine Hepburn, Bette Davis, and Joan Crawford in the 1930s were often intelligent but needed men alternately to tame and to soften them. And at the other end of the spectrum, in the dancing movies of Ginger Rogers and Fred Astaire, it was often Rogers who played the responsible, capable, working woman, and Astaire whose devil-may-care ways needed reforming. Their movies usually ended not with blissful domestic life for her but with successful professional partnership for them both.

How were women to understand their roles through these films? Were they to go from the free but irresponsible flapper to the sub-

The Chez Marie beauty parlor in Miami, Florida, did a thriving business. Working in a beauty salon was one job that women could do without fear that they would be taking opportunities away from men.

In The Philadelphia Story *(1936), Katharine Hepburn portrays a wealthy, strong, intelligent, independent, and responsible (if repressed) divorcée. She ultimately remarries her wealthy ex-husband (Cary Grant) once he abandons alcohol, gets a job, and shows her that she, too, has foibles.*

missive, nurturing wife who could lighten the burden of dark days but stay safely in her place? Or was there another model still available? It was, after all, in the 1930s that Babe Didrikson emerged as a sports hero, winning two gold medals at the 1932 Olympics, in javelin and hurdles, and a silver in the high jump, and eschewing all feminine wiles. She excelled at every sport she tried, including baseball and basketball, and won a diving championship and tournaments in tennis and golf. According to *Newsweek*, when asked what she did best, she drawled, "I'm best at everything." The media often portrayed Didrikson as a sort of freak, and she earned her living in the 1930s by traveling through the countryside exhibiting her skills, drawing crowds who wanted to see the unusual. Unusual she may have been, but she was also undeniably strong and independent and highly visible.

Babe Didrikson won the silver medal for the high jump at the 1932 Olympics. She also won two gold medals, for javelin and hurdles. As a world-class athlete, she offered women a role model that defied the values of both the flapper and the nurturing wife.

In the depths of the depression, with society as well as the economy seeming to teeter on the brink of disaster, women found they were expected to be both competent and submissive, independent enough to survive, but unthreatening. What society demanded of women in the 1930s was complex and contradictory, but it did not completely erode the image of confident, competent, public womanhood created in the 1920s.

MANAGERS TRYOUT THEATRE

A DIVISION OF THE FEDERAL THEATRE
PRESENTS

A WOMAN OF DESTINY

A NEW PLAY BY
SAMUEL JESSE WARSHAWSKY
WITH
ALEXANDRA CARLISLE
and a Broadway Cast of 40

ORCHESTRA 55¢
MEZZANINE 25¢
BALCONY 15¢

EVENINGS 8:40
MAT. SAT. 2:40
NO PERFORMANCE MON.

WILLIS THEATRE

138 th St. AND WILLIS AVE, BRONX

CHAPTER 7

WOMEN AND THE NEW DEAL

In the 1920s, Emily Newell Blair had turned from free-lance writing and suffrage movement work to Democratic politics. A graduate of Goucher College, married and the mother of two children, she had risen in the ranks to become national vice-chairman of the Democratic party. Blair set up 30 "schools of democracy" to train the new women voters and advocated the election of women as regular party politicians, not as part of a separate women's politics. But she found the system more stubborn than she had anticipated.

Blair retired from party office in 1928 and three years later wrote an article entitled "Why I Am Discouraged about Women in Politics." "Now at the end of ten years of suffrage," she confessed, "I find politics still a male monopoly. It is hardly easier for women to get themselves elected to office than it was before the Equal Suffrage Amendment was passed. Women still have little part in framing political policies and determining party tactics." Indeed, Blair claimed that women had less of a voice in party leadership than they had in 1920, when, as an unknown quantity, they had been courted by male politicians.

In the 1930s, few women held elected office. Of the dozen women who served in Congress at some point during the decade, only two were active on women's issues. Blair lamented, "Unfortunately for feminism, it was agreed to drop the sex line in politics. And it was

A poster for a 1936 production of A Woman of Destiny *in New York, sponsored by the Federal Theatre, a New Deal agency. The play tells the story of a woman antiwar activist who becomes President.*

In Kansas City, Missouri, Eleanor Roosevelt inspects loom workers in a project sponsored by the Works Progress Administration.

dropped by the women. Even those who ran for office forgot that they were women."

Yet the 1930s did see a dramatic increase in women's political influence. This increase came through appointed, rather than elected, offices. It came as the fruit of Franklin Delano Roosevelt's program, the New Deal that he promised Americans when they elected him President in 1932. The increase in influence was also the result of his wife Eleanor's strong and deeply rooted networks among women reformers and her political abilities as a shaper of New Deal policy.

By early 1933, when Roosevelt took office, the depression was four years old. Herbert Hoover, elected President in 1928, had hesitated to intervene drastically in the economy. Hoover had created public works projects that erected large dams but employed few workers. He had provided some support for banks and had said many encouraging things, but the economy went from bad to worse. In 1929, the giant U.S. Steel Corporation had employed 224,980 full-time workers. In 1931, it employed only 53,619; in 1932, 18,958; and in 1933, none at all. It had turned all its remaining employees into half-time workers. In 1933, more than 1,000 foreclosures a day ousted families from their homes. Even renters were not immune. In New York City, landlords initiated more than 54,700 eviction proceedings in the first two months of 1933.

An outdoor soup kitchen in New York in 1932. Unemployment increased as the Great Depression continued under the administration of Herbert Hoover.

Faced with declining opportunities and increased racial hostility, 10,000 Puerto Ricans headed for home, and many Chinese returned to China. Unable to create jobs or to meet the needs of the unemployed, officials in the Southwest closed ranks against Mexicans and Mexican Americans, accusing them of stealing jobs and using up relief dollars. In 1932, officials in Los Angeles rounded up all the Mexicans they could find, put them and their American-born children in boxcars, and sent them to Mexico. In all, across the United States, these deportations affected approximately 400,000 Mexicans. They solved nothing. Indeed, many "Mexicans" on relief roles were, in fact, U.S. citizens, born and raised on this side of the border. To the officials responsible, however, they all looked alike.

Many Chicanos made their way to the cities in search of opportunities or help. They were joined by 400,000 African Americans migrating from the South to the North for the same reason. And farmers who had lost their homes, along with tenant farmers unable to get leases, rolled west, as one observer noted, "like a parade." Whole counties hit the road.

The cities offered no respite from the hard times. In 1933, half the workers in Cleveland were unemployed, as well as 80 percent of those in Toledo. Average family income plummeted from $2,300 in 1929 to $1,500 in 1933. In 1932, 28 percent of U.S. households had no employed worker at all. Even those who had work suffered. Stenographers in New York who had made $40 a week in 1929 were making only $16 four years later. Most working women in Chicago

A social worker at a settlement house tries to find a job for her client; other volunteers offer milk to children. Eleanor Roosevelt got her start in public service by working in a settlement house in New York.

earned less than 25 cents an hour. Unable to pay their teachers, school districts cut school to three days a week, to two months a year, or simply closed them altogether, depriving a third of a million children of school in 1932.

People looked to Roosevelt's administration to make order of the chaos, to reopen the banks and schools, and to put people back to work. In the process of accomplishing these tasks, the Roosevelts and their allies changed the relationship between individuals and the government. With her long history of work in social welfare, Eleanor Roosevelt stood at the center of that change.

Anna Eleanor Roosevelt had been born into an old, wealthy, and distinguished New York family. But by the time Eleanor was 10, both her parents had died—her mother after an operation and her father essentially from alcoholism. She spent the rest of her childhood with relatives. When she reached 15, she was sent to a London boarding school.

When Roosevelt returned to New York to enter high society, she plunged into social service activities. At the age of 18, she worked at the Rivington Street Settlement House, teaching calisthenics and dancing to the impoverished neighbors. She also joined the National Consumers' League, which used the power of consumers to try to better the conditions of workers, particularly women. Employers who met the Consumers' League standards could use the League label, and consumers could buy the goods they produced knowing they had been produced under decent conditions. Roosevelt visited the clothing factories and sweatshops that the League targeted and never forgot what she saw.

At the same time, she had fallen in love with her cousin, Franklin Roosevelt, an ambitious young Harvard graduate. They married in March 1905. For the next 10 years she was either pregnant or recovering from pregnancy. Eleanor helped Franklin's early political career by organizing and hosting social and political gatherings. Then, in 1917, she discovered that her husband was having an affair with her trusted friend, Lucy Mercer. Devastated, she offered him a divorce, but a divorce would have ruined his political career and deprived him of a valued friend and partner. The couple reconciled, and both plunged into politics.

Even the setback of Franklin's lifelong paralysis from a polio attack in 1921 could not stop the Roosevelts. During the 1920s, Franklin played an ever-increasing role in the Democratic party, and Eleanor joined reform organizations, including the Women's Trade Union League. She discovered in the women reformers a warm, supportive network of friends and an astute set of politicians. This warmth sustained her in the rough and tumble political world. In particular, her intimate relationship with journalist Lorena Hickok provided the essential emotional support she could no longer get from her husband. In turn, as early as 1924, the women reformers saw Eleanor Roosevelt as a major leader. By 1928, she expressed her frustration that these women politicians met with so few rewards. She would carry this sense of politics and reform—and this network of women—with her into the White House in 1933.

The women who would join Eleanor Roosevelt in Washington were not new to politics. In overlapping networks, they had been building connections and careers throughout the 1910s and 1920s. For example, Mary W. Dewson started her career in Massachusetts reform and suffrage circles. In the 1920s in New York, she served as the civic secretary of the Women's City Club and the research secretary of the National Consumers' League. In these positions, she worked with women from the Women's Trade

The National Consumers' League urged women shoppers to buy clothes with the League's label. Manufacturers could use the label only if they provided good working conditions and observed labor laws that protected women employees.

Union League, the League of Women Voters, the YWCA, and other organizations.

By 1929, Dewson knew all the leading women reformers in the city. With these connections in mind, Eleanor recruited her into Democratic politics in 1928, and from 1932 to 1934 Dewson headed the party's Women's Division. By 1937, she served as vice chairman of the Democratic National Committee and on a number of government advisory boards. Dewson wanted to use political appointments both to get nonpartisan women reformers into the government and to reward loyal Democratic women. For his part, Franklin Roosevelt wanted to be the first President to appoint a woman to the cabinet. In Frances Perkins he found an ideal candidate.

Perkins had connections to both political and reform networks. She had graduated from Mount Holyoke College in 1902, worked in settlement houses in Chicago, and then studied and conducted research for her master's degree in sociology and economics at Columbia University. She had worked for the Consumers' League as a lobbyist. In 1918, Governor Al Smith appointed her to the New York State Industrial Commission. In 1928, the new governor, Franklin Roosevelt, appointed Perkins Industrial Commissioner, a promotion. After he was elected President, Roosevelt agreed to nominate

As the first woman to serve as U.S. secretary of labor, Frances Perkins dealt with skeptical male workers and often hostile employers. In one city, officials chased her from site to site when she tried to meet with the workers. She finally held her meeting on the steps of the post office—a federal building over which city officials had no control.

Perkins as secretary of labor, and Dewson launched a nationwide campaign in her support.

Yet Perkins hesitated to leave her friends and the job she loved to face the publicity and the cost of moving to Washington. Dewson had little patience with such concerns. "You owe it to the women," Perkins remembered her saying. "Don't be such a baby, Frances. You do the right thing. I'll murder you if you don't."

Other women received posts in every agency from the diplomatic corps and the U.S. Mint to the Consumers' Advisory Board of the National Recovery Administration (NRA), an economic agency that was part of the New Deal program. Under Roosevelt, a higher percentage of women received government appointments than ever before, except during World War I.

Women fared best in new agencies. In the seven newest New Deal agencies, including the Social Security Board, the Works Progress Administration, and the Home Owners' Loan Corporation, women made up 44.4 percent of the employees in 1939. The 10 executive departments were another story. In the Departments of Labor, State, and Interior, women constituted more than one-third of the employees, but in the Departments of War, Navy, Commerce, and the Post Office, they ranged from 15.2 percent to only 5.5 percent of employees.

Eleanor Roosevelt (right) supported Mary McLeod Bethune in her fight to advance the rights of women and African Americans. Roosevelt also encouraged her husband to respond to the concerns of blacks.

There were some women who had built up political networks over the previous decades whose networks touched, rather than over-lapped, those of Eleanor Roosevelt and Mary Dewson. Mary McLeod Bethune was one such woman. Born in South Carolina in the mid-1870s, the 15th of 17 children, she was the one chosen to attend school and teach the others. A determined mother and scholarships helped Bethune, who was proud of her African heritage, attend a seminary, a bible school, and a number of mission schools in pursuit of her desire to be a missionary in Africa.

During her training, Bethune married and had a child. As her efforts to go to Africa failed, she realized that her true mission was in the United States. With great faith, and $1.50, she started a school for girls in Daytona, Florida. In 1915, the first class of five students graduated. By 1927, the school had buildings and property worth more than $1 million. In 1929, it became Bethune-Cookman College.

But Bethune's activities ranged far beyond her school. A vital force in women's clubs, in 1924 she was elected president of the National Association of Colored Women (NACW). Like all Bethune's organizations, it had a large vision, working to secure a federal antilynching bill, helping rural women and women in industry, training clerks and typists, and raising the status of women in the Philippines, Puerto Rico, Haiti, and Africa.

Bethune knew that the number of black women graduating from college was increasing but that the status of black working women had declined in depression conditions. She wanted to mobilize the power of college women on behalf of the others. She felt frustrated with the lack of progress, the conservatism of the NACW, and the difficulties of working in mixed-race organizations such as the Association of Southern Women for the Prevention of Lynching. There, when push came to shove, white members had refused to support a federal antilynching law, claiming it violated states' rights. Though Bethune remained more friendly to such groups than did many black women leaders, she decided to found her own organization.

On December 5, 1935, Bethune held the founding meeting of the National Council of Negro Women at the Harlem branch of the YWCA. "Most people think I am a dreamer," she told her audience at that meeting. "Through dreams many things have come true. I am interested in women and I believe in their possibilities. . . . We need vision for larger things." Although many prominent black women

Mary McLeod Bethune (front row, center) formed the National Council of Negro Women in 1935 because she believed black women needed their own organization.

doubted the need for such an organization, Bethune insisted that black women needed their own group, an umbrella organization for their own clubs and associations. The National Association of Colored Women, by contrast, was affiliated with the National Council of Women, which had, she explained, "forty-three organizations with only one Negro organization and we have no specific place on their program. . . . We need an organization to open new doors for our young women [which] when [it] speaks, its power will be felt." The doubters joined.

Bethune's stature had led to her involvement in national-level politics. In 1928, she had participated in the White House Conference on Child Welfare. Yet the New Deal was slow to call on her. As late as 1929, Franklin Roosevelt had boasted that he had never lunched with an African American. He ignored NAACP requests to support a civil rights platform. African Americans supported Roosevelt only because of his job creation and welfare programs. Then, in 1934, Eleanor Roosevelt began taking public stands on racial issues. Unlike her husband, she lent her public support to the antilynching bill. Finally, in 1936, when Roosevelt won 76 percent of the black vote, he responded with black political appointments.

The press called the new appointees the "Black Cabinet." Bethune was among them. She directed the Negro Division of the National Youth Administration (NYA), whose mandate was to find jobs for people between the ages of 16 and 24. Bethune soon made her mark. Seeing the Black Cabinet divided by internal disputes, she organized its members into the Federal Council of Negro Affairs, whose aim was to achieve consensus on policy issues. She also made certain that black universities benefited from the NYA, implementing a small, special scholarship fund for African-American college students because of their greater need. In the 1930s, 48 percent of the fathers of black college students worked in unskilled, low-paying jobs; only 4.7 percent of white students' fathers did.

Many black southern women with fewer connections, less education, and less power than Bethune, who were surrounded by the terrorist, racist activities of the Ku Klux Klan, felt they had no choice but to repress their anger and resentment in order to keep their jobs and provide for their families. Bethune would have to express their feelings for them. She did not hesitate. In a typical moment, she

Franklin Roosevelt appointed Mary McLeod Bethune to direct the Negro Division of the National Youth Administration in 1936.

wrote to Secretary of War Henry L. Stimson on learning that the War Department had failed to invite black women to a 1941 conference on organizing women for the war effort, "We are not humiliated. We are incensed."

Together these women, black and white, tried to ensure that other women benefited from New Deal programs. They were consummate lobbyists. Eleanor Roosevelt had unprecedented access to policymakers, addressing committees of the House of Representatives, conferring with committee chairmen, and sending members of Congress letters demanding the appointment of a coordinator of child care—all the while claiming to act only as a private citizen.

Meanwhile, real private citizens across the country were appealing personally to Eleanor for help. In 1934, a young, pregnant woman from Eureka, California, wrote, "Dear Mrs. Roosevelt, I know you are overburdened with requests for help. . . . But I am not asking for myself alone. It is as a potential mother and as one woman to another." With both Eleanor and Franklin, ordinary Americans felt a new intimacy. This was true even before Franklin began his regular

This Boston exhibition of works by women painters was one of many Works Progress Administration projects that employed artists.

informal radio talks, called "fireside chats," and Eleanor began writing her newspaper column, "My Day," which first appeared in December 1935 and reached an audience of more than 4 million. In her column, she discussed not only homey issues, such as entertaining and family dinners, and more exotic experiences, such as royal receptions or trips, but political issues as well. While the public felt they really got to know Eleanor's private life, she used the column to educate her readers and promote New Deal policies.

With public charities running dry and states going bankrupt, the federal government swept in like a benign wind. The New Deal created massive temporary job programs and provided relief payments, first through the Federal Relief Administration (FERA), which was created in March 1933 with $500 million, and the Public Works Administration (PWA), which funded major construction projects with $3.3 billion. Then, in the desperate winter of 1933–34, the Civil Works Administration (CWA) was established; it hired 2.6 million people within a month. At its peak in January 1934, the CWA employed more than 4 million people with wages averaging about $15 per week, twice the usual FERA rate. When the depression lingered, at Roosevelt's request Congress passed the Emergency Relief Act, under which Roosevelt created the Works Progress Administration (WPA) with the largest single financial appropriation to that date, $4.88 billion, in order to create jobs.

The New Deal also attempted a more permanent restructuring of the economy. In 1933, the Agricultural Adjustment Act (AAA) and the National Industrial Recovery Act (NIRA), which created the National Recovery Administration (NRA), tried to stabilize production on farms and in factories. These agencies tried to ensure decent working conditions by bringing consumers, employers, and workers together to create codes for the industries and prices and quotas for the farmers. They also made it harder for employers to discriminate against workers for joining a union.

These measures were so popular that when the Supreme Court declared the laws unconstitutional in 1935 and 1936, new, more carefully drafted laws swiftly replaced the major provisions of the AAA and the provisions of the NIRA that protected workers' rights.

New Deal programs brought relief to Hispanic families in New Mexico, where the depression had reduced the availability of work for men and where the drought prevented women from growing enough food for their families. Even with New Deal aid, some families were forced to move on.

Industrial codes were abandoned, but in 1938 the Fair Labor Standards Act legislated minimum wages and maximum hours, and this time the Supreme Court let the act stand.

The federal government also entered more permanently and more broadly into social welfare, making the United States the last industrial nation to do so. Finally, the United States, like most European countries, had unemployment insurance, old age insurance (Social Security), and aid to dependent children. The last was a provision of the 1935 Social Security Act drafted by the reformers Grace Abbott and Katherine Lenroot, who headed the Children's Bureau. For the first time, the U.S. government became a major guarantor of family welfare.

Some of these programs greatly benefited women; others had mixed and often unexpected consequences. New Deal programs employed countless numbers of women. They also kept many women in college; 45 percent of the college students helped by the NYA in 1936–37 were women. The number of women in college rose almost as fast as the number of men, from 480,000 in 1930 to 601,000 in 1940.

For many women, New Deal programs made the difference between starvation and survival. In northern New Mexico, Mexican-American families had survived by a combination of migrant male labor on farms, in mines, or on the railroads, and with food grown by women for their own families. The depression had reduced the availability of men's jobs, and drought diminished the agricultural yield. Unable to pay their taxes, 65 percent of the local farmers faced possible eviction. Families shared what food they had, but it was not enough. By mid-decade, 60 percent of the Mexican Americans in northern New Mexican villages were hanging on only with government aid. In some villages, every family appeared on the relief list.

The New Deal programs could also provide the margin between despair and self-respect. Stella Boone and Ethel Stringer took time out from their new jobs as WPA Adult Education teachers at a Hispanic secondary school in San Antonio to write to Eleanor Roosevelt in 1936. "Many of us were desperate," they explained, "the unhappy victims of circumstances over which we had no control. . . . It is unalterably true that shabbiness and hunger are the foes of self-respect. With our homes broken, our children scattered, our souls torn with anguish and desperation. . . . Some of us had lost our homes which were nearly paid for, had sold our furniture, piece by piece, our jewelry, and even most of our clothes. . . . Just when all seemed lost and maddened by grief and fear we were ready for anything, this Adult Educational Program came, providing us with a means of livelihood, a ladder up which we could climb again to patriotism and self-respect."

In such programs, Hispanic and Anglo women in San Antonio studied business and clerical subjects in the hope of obtaining white-collar employment. With its vast bureaucracy, the New Deal did provide many clerical and professional jobs throughout the government. At the state level, women ran the WPA's Division of Women's Work. They also participated in the WPA's writing, music, and theater projects. Anthropologist and Harlem Renaissance novelist Zora Neale Hurston collected folklore from African Americans in Florida for the WPA Writers Project. Photographers Dorothea Lange and Marion Post Wolcott took pictures for the Farm Security Administration. Other women worked in government-funded positions in

Some WPA adult education programs taught both traditional academic skills, as in the Georgia school at left. Others, such as the Denver, Colorado, school above, taught people to weave. The clothing made by the students was given to relief recipients.

hospitals, nursery schools, and cafeterias. They cleaned public buildings and organized city records.

Most women's work projects consisted, however, of sewing rooms, where workers made garments for relief recipients; food processing, such as canning factories; health care; and domestic-service training programs. In San Antonio, for example, by early 1936, the WPA employed 1,280 women and just over twice that many men (2,739) in professional projects. On the other hand, a single sewing room in that city employed 2,300 people. In the country as a whole, 56 percent of the women employed by the WPA worked in sewing rooms.

New Deal policies focused on promoting domestic roles for women, such as sewing, cleaning, canning, and nursing. Administrators tended to see women as temporary workers who were helping out in an emergency and would return to the home after the depression. Why teach them nondomestic skills they would never use again? Operating procedures in the WPA mandated that job preference be given to male family heads or, if none existed, to adult male children in the household. Only if a husband were ab-sent or disabled and no adult sons lived at home could women receive a high priority at the agency. Even in the National Youth Administration, men received preference over women in job placement. The WPA limited

Hispanic women work for a WPA weaving project in New Mexico. The government's Spanish Colonial Arts program was among the first to recognize the value of cultural diversity.

the proportion of jobs it opened to women to between 12 and 16 percent.

There were other limits to the New Deal programs. Social Security excluded domestic servants and agricultural workers, and by doing so excluded from its benefits most black female and Chicana workers. In the 1930s, 90 percent of black women worked in agricultural labor or domestic service. No code and, later, no minimum wage or maximum hours law covered these workers, either.

Nor was government relief evenly distributed. It went disproportionately to whites. Black women in the South and Chicanas in the Southwest found themselves ousted from work relief programs so that they would have to take poorly paid domestic work or labor in the cotton or vegetable and fruit fields. In addition, the New Deal's crop reduction policies, geared toward increasing agricultural prices by reducing supply, led landowners to evict large numbers of black women who had raised crops on their land as tenants or sharecroppers, splitting the yield with the landowner.

The administrators of government programs were overwhelmingly white. They had little interest in creating jobs programs that would pull women of color away from domestic service. And they were thoroughly imbued with the racial attitudes that dominated their regions. In 1935, *Opportunity,* the journal of the Urban League, an organization whose purpose was to better the condition of African Americans, quoted a Georgia black woman who complained, "When I go to them for help they talk to me like I was a dog." Some government officials simply refused relief to black or Chicano clients. Mosel Brinson of Georgia wrote to the U.S. Department of Agriculture in 1935, "I am a widow woman with seven head of children, and I live on my place with a plenty of help. All are good workers and I wants to farm. I has no mule, no wagon, no feed, no grocery, and these women and men that is controlling the Civil Work for the Government won't help me." She added a telling postscript: "P.S. These poor white people that lives around me wants the colored people to work for them for nothing and if you won't do that they goes down to the relief office and tell the women,—'don't help the colored people, we will give them plenty of work to do, but they won't work.'"

In Greenwood, Mississippi, the white women who administered federal work relief told elderly black widows to go hunt for washing. Pinkie Pilcher wrote to the White House about it in 1936: "The white people dont pay anything for their washing. [A black woman] cant do enough washing to feed her family."

Yet white program directors continued to create programs that channeled women of color into domestic service. Mary Katherine Dickson, who administered federal relief programs in San Antonio in 1937, complained that "the majority of housewives in San Antonio have a very real servant problem on their hands and, at present, no means of solving it satisfactorily." She offered her proposal

Working for the Farm Security Administration, photographer Arthur Rothstein took this shot of black sharecroppers leaving their farm in Missouri after being evicted.

Federal relief programs aimed at helping black women and Chicanas were often designed to keep them in domestic service.

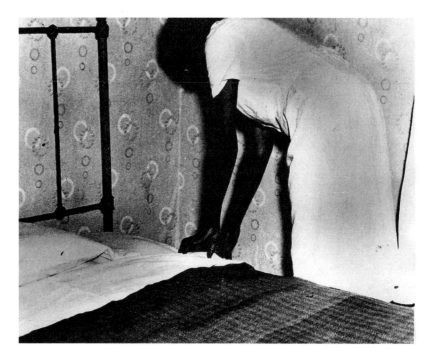

for training black adults in domestic service as the best solution to their unemployment and white housewives' needs, because "between 75% and 85% of persons employed in household service are black." She condemned the public school system for providing the same curriculum and the same expectations for black and white students.

In Denver, officials found they could not fill the classes they had created to train Chicanas in domestic service. Chicanas and black women found almost any other kind of work preferable. Some of these women benefited from New Deal–sponsored classes in clerical skills, but most avoided domestic work by finding jobs in WPA sewing rooms.

In some locations, even the sewing rooms discriminated. In Fayetteville, North Carolina, officials closed the sewing project and opened a cleaning project for black women. And, unlike white women, black women in the WPA were often assigned to heavy outdoor labor. A physician in Florence, South Carolina, complained to the WPA in 1936 of a "beautification" project where "women are worked in 'gangs' in connection with the City's dump pile, incinerator and ditch piles."

Other programs not particularly aimed at women also could have unexpected results. The Indian Reorganization Act of 1934 aimed to give Native American tribes increased autonomy by creating tribal governments built around newly written constitutions. Although the underlying sentiment of the act was a new respect for tribal cultures, the new constitutions tended to be built on white models. In tribes where women had been excluded from formal political participation, they gained new voting power, and new women leaders emerged. On the other hand, in some other tribes, women lost economic rights and political power, as they did among the Iroquois, where women had had the power as a group to depose chiefs and influence tribal decisions. Moreover, among the Navajo, New Deal policies of reducing stock in the name of conserving overgrazed land lessened the economic power of women, who were the traditional tribal stock owners. At the same time, jobs programs favoring men made the Navajo men less dependent economically on the clan's women and less willing to contribute their income to the extended family.

Even the industrial codes aimed at improving work conditions could backfire. Wages increased rapidly. Between July 1933 and August 1934, southern women textile workers doubled their hourly wages, a more rapid increase than the men's. Even so, however, the $12 a week they now received would scarcely make ends meet. Besides, most received only three-fourths of that amount because, to meet code requirements regarding the number of work hours per week, many mills closed every fourth week. Short hours and production cuts undermined women's wage advances. Increased demands for productivity, on the other hand, made a mockery of the reduction to an eight-hour day. Higher wages could also lead to mechanization and layoffs as machines became cheaper than human workers. In 1935, a black woman worker told an NRA investigator, "They laid off one-fourth of the people in my room after the last raise we got."

Secretary of Labor Frances Perkins may not have been entirely satisfied with the treatment women got from the New Deal. In her papers at the National Archives there is an unsigned, unattributed, undated "Resolution on Unemployment and Working Women." According to that document, "They have been thrown out of jobs as married women, refused relief as single women, discriminated against

A Native American mother and child rest in a Minnesota blueberry camp sponsored by the Farm Security Administration. The fact that New Deal agencies provided more and better-paying jobs to men than to women often altered the balance of power between men and women.

by the N.R.A. and ignored by the C.W.A." Pondering these issues in 1935, writer and editor Genevieve Parkhurst wondered in *Harper's* magazine whether feminism was dead. After all, almost one-fourth of the NRA codes established wage rates for women that were 14 percent to 30 percent lower than those for men. And southern codes for laundries established earnings for black laundresses below precode levels.

The emphasis throughout the Roosevelt administration, including that of Eleanor Roosevelt and Frances Perkins, remained on providing male workers with jobs and supporting families. Single women earners were invisible; married women workers existed only as mothers or wives. WPA rules prohibited the agency from providing work for women eligible for aid from the Aid to Dependent Children program as well as for most married women. Such policies aimed at curbing the seeming trend of women becoming the family breadwinner; if there was no man to do so, the role would be assumed by the state.

With the tremendous anxiety over social stability, and fears for the family as the institution at the core of social order, few spoke for the woman workers, and feminist individualism was rarely seen. In 1935, the *New York Herald Tribune* reported that the president of the national League of Women Voters, the organizational heir to the suffrage movement, was defining "a 1935 new-style feminism." This new feminism, she insisted, did not demand that women disappear into their kitchens. Instead, it required "women making good in positions of responsibility, other women backing them up, and all preparing themselves for similar service," as they did in Roosevelt's administration. Yet the new focus was less on personal achievement than it had been in the 1920s. Women social reformers had achieved high visibility and power with the New Deal, and those focusing instead on equal rights for women were in disarray.

The social reformers saw themselves as bettering the world for women, helping women and children fend off economic disaster, fostering the success of women in government positions, and safeguarding the welfare of working women. But in Frances Perkins's Department of Labor, the Children's Bureau expanded rapidly, while the Women's Bureau remained small. That policy decision left childless women stranded and left little room for a notion of women's rights that did not depend on their family roles. Despite its powerful women, the New Deal did not revolutionize the position of women in relation to men or the family.

For all its contradictions, however, the New Deal had drastically changed the relationship of women to the state. By providing Social Security, however limited, unemployment insurance, jobs, NRA hearings where workers could air their grievances directly to federal officials, wage and hour legislation, and other programs, the New Deal altered what people believed they could expect and took new responsibility for the welfare of families and workers. These heightened expectations, particularly among working-class women, led them to take matters into their own hands.

CONTEMPORARY JUSTICE AND WOMAN

CHAPTER 8

TAKING MATTERS INTO THEIR OWN HANDS

Throughout the 1930s, impoverished and unemployed people found that those from whom they sought help—charity agents, local, state, and federal officials, and employers—all sought to define their needs, aims, and the limits of their aspirations. The black women and Chicanas who wrote to the Roosevelts and to the WPA protesting their treatment were among the women who resisted such definitions. They insisted on defining their own needs, desires, and identities. Many went beyond writing letters. They joined together, sometimes with men, sometimes without them, to protest as a community and to take matters into their own hands.

In journalist Caroline Bird's memoir of the Great Depression, *The Invisible Scar,* she recalled, "Eviction was so common that children in a Philadelphia day-care center made a game of it. They would pile all the doll furniture up first in one corner and then in another." Rents dropped precipitously during the 1930s, but however low they fell, unemployed workers could not afford to pay them. Tired of moving, desperate for housing and self-respect, they began to fight the evictions.

Women played a central role in eviction protests. It was women who had built up neighborhood networks over the years, visiting, sharing work with and caring for neighbors, gossiping, distributing

Contemporary Justice and Woman, a painting by Emil Bisttram in the Department of Justice building in Washington, D.C., is the only New Deal-sponsored art that depicts the woman suffrage movement. Women used the right to vote as a springboard to a greater role in all aspects of public life.

An evicted woman in Chicago. Although rents fell drastically in the 1930s, the unemployed still could not afford to pay them, and evictions were frequent.

home work, and taking in boarders. Women had called on these networks before when their roles as providers and nurturers had been threatened. As recently as the second decade of the century, they had rioted over meat prices. Now these women's neighborhood networks were matched by newer networks of unemployed men. The men, too, organized on the basis of neighborhoods. With the help of the Communist party, they united into Unemployed Councils. These councils organized the bulk of the eviction protests, but it was the neighborhood networks that made them successful.

In cities as different as New York, Baltimore, and Sioux City, Iowa, women and men would gather up the neighborhood and march to a site where a city official, on behalf of a landlord, had just thrown a family into the street. Vastly outnumbered, the city official could only leave or watch helplessly as the crowd took the tenant's belongings back into the apartment. Eviction proceedings took two or three months, which gave unemployed tenants valuable breathing space before the city marshal would again appear to evict them.

Women also mobilized their neighborhoods to fight for more relief. Willye Jeffries, an African-American woman who had organized tenants in the 1930s, told reporter Studs Terkel for his book *Hard Times* about a time when relief workers refused to provide $100 toward the burial expenses of an old lady. Jeffries explained, "We got a crowd of about fifty people and went down to the station. We gonna stay until we get this hundred dollars for this old lady." After staying two or three days and being threatened with arrest, they finally found the man in charge and secured the money.

Jeffries's neighborhood organizations were mixed racially and ethnically, as were the neighborhoods. "There were a lot of Polish women in this organization, too," she told Terkel. When the police tried to stop their protests and picketing, the Polish women "had cayenne pepper, and they threw it in those policemen's eyes, and nobody knew who done it, but they went blind." In such protests, Jeffries concluded, "The women, they played the biggest roles."

Although men made most of the street-corner speeches, women maintained the picket lines. They did so even when, as the Communist paper the *Daily Worker* reported in 1933 about a Brownsville, New York, rent protest, "day after day thugs and police beat women and children who picketed in front of the house." Black women organized neighborhood Housewives Leagues over jobs as well as housing. Discrimination ran rampant in the job market, and many employers refused to hire African Americans. In Chicago, Baltimore,

A meeting of the Communist party in Detroit, Michigan. Throughout the country, the Communist party helped women and men organize neighborhood organizations to fight evictions and gain relief for the unemployed.

Mary McLeod Bethune joins a demonstration against People's Drugstore in Washington, D.C., which refused to employ black clerks. At right, the women's auxiliary to the United Auto Workers Association demonstrates in Flint, Michigan, to demand equal pay for equal work.

Detroit, Harlem, and Cleveland, Housewives Leagues used their power as consumers to launch "Don't Buy Where You Can't Work" campaigns. Stores in black neighborhoods would either have to employ black workers or lose black business. These boycotts resulted in as many as 75,000 new jobs for blacks during the 1930s.

Women also took the power of their neighborhood networks beyond their own streets. As members of women's auxiliaries to largely male unions, they played a vital role in supporting the major men's labor strikes of the decade, including the Minneapolis general strike and the Flint, Michigan, sit-down strike at General Motors. But the women also organized on their own behalf, as workers.

In 1933, in St. Louis, Missouri, 900 black women pecan workers walked out of seven factories owned by the same man. They demanded higher pay and better working conditions—pay and conditions equal to those of white women workers. Connie Smith, a middle-aged black woman, led the protest, and she secured widespread cooperation, including that of the Unemployed Councils. When the factory owner tried to pit whites against blacks by offering white women a wage increase if they would return to work, a group of 1,500 black and white women marched together to City Hall to refuse the offer. Faced with solidarity between black and white women, the owner surrendered on all counts—equal treatment, higher wages, and better conditions.

Determined to take advantage of the ferment, in 1934 William Green, head of the American Federation of Labor (AFL), announced a campaign to bring women into the unions. Yet just bringing them in as members did not guarantee them a voice in policy-making. At Philco, the nation's leading radio maker and Philadelphia's largest single employer, even with the union, women and men had different assignments and were subject to different wage rates. Although women made up about half of Philco's six to seven thousand employees and half the union members of the United Electrical, Radio and Machine Workers of America, men held the offices, including those in departments with large female majorities.

Few women protested the distribution of labor. As former worker Catherine McGill told an interviewer, "At that time, you were glad to have a job." And most of Philco's women workers believed that some jobs were more appropriate to women and others to men. They accepted that those jobs labeled "women's jobs" had lower wages.

In the 1930s, most factory jobs were divided into women's work and men's work. Women's work, such as sewing clothes, usually paid less than the jobs reserved for men.

Strikers in New York City in 1937. The CIO, which organized union workers by industry rather than by skills, included women in its membership but often discriminated against them nevertheless.

Ironically, at Philco this acceptance of jobs and wages defined by sex, which had started as a way to keep women from competing for "men's jobs," resulted in men losing jobs to women after all. An unsuccessful strike by the union at the end of 1937 led to a reclassification of 1,500 positions from "men's jobs" to "women's jobs" at correspondingly lower pay, and women became the majority of workers at the plant.

In the same year that Green announced his policy shift, the International Ladies' Garment Workers Union (ILGWU) began organizing women workers in San Antonio. They struggled to unite Anglo and Mexican-American women factory workers with the largely Chicana hand sewers and embroiderers who worked at home. Unfortunately, the enormous amount of unemployment in the city made it easy for employers to fire or otherwise harass union members and replace them. No lasting success was achieved until 1935, when New Deal legislation made such company harassment of union members illegal. From 1936 to 1938, the union helped garment factory workers make steady gains in San Antonio.

The changes in labor legislation fostered dramatic growth in union membership and the formation of a new Committee on Industrial Organization of the American Federation of Labor. It soon split off, amid bitter disputes, to become the Congress of Industrial Organizations (CIO). The CIO proved more hospitable to women workers because it organized by industry (all steel workers, or all automobile workers) rather than by skills (such as carpenters or machinists, categories from which women had often been excluded).

Of course, this shift did not change the prevalent ideas about men's and women's work overnight, and even CIO unions approved settlements with employers that allowed lower wages for women than for men in the same jobs. Stella Nowicki, an organizer in Chicago meat-packing plants at the time, recalled, "Women had an awfully tough time in the union because the men brought their prejudices there." Moreover, after a day's work many women still had to care for children, make meals, and clean the house. "The union didn't encourage women to come to meetings," Nowicki said. "They didn't actually want to take up the problems that women had." And most women workers remained in fields that were hardly touched by union organization.

Yet over the course of the decade women's union membership tripled, reaching 800,000 by 1940. Two hundred thousand of them were in the ILGWU, but women also organized in a wide variety of occupations and industries, from domestic work to clerical work, canning to radio manufacturing. Often the women were hungry for unions. United, they had a chance to take some control over the conditions of their work and livelihoods. Instead of depending solely on their employers, they could depend on each other and bargain with their employers.

Despite continued wage inequities, the unions, new legislation, and federal attempts at regulating the workplace gave women workers an expanded vision of their rights. They had a sense that their government would hear them and act. In NRA hearings, for example, women complained again and again about sexual harassment. In textile mills, men used profane and vulgar language, which the women found humiliating and degrading. Worse yet, bosses pressured young women workers into sexual relations and fired them if they did not comply. Mothers who tried to protect their daughters were turned away and told it was none of their business. These issues still lay outside the formal codes and contracts affecting workers. Women used these new forums to make this hidden abuse, this particularly female problem, visible and to demand remedies.

Sexual harassment was one of the shared experiences that bound cannery workers at the California Sanitary Canning Company (Cal San) together. In 1939, during a record-breaking heat wave, nearly all 430 women workers, most of them Mexican Americans, walked off their fruit-canning jobs.

The tremendous solidarity of this union local was built on ethnic, kinship, and neighborhood as well as gender lines. Sometimes three generations of women worked in the plant. They shared the experience of slippery floors, itchy peach fuzz, and the ever-swifter pace of production, in addition to sexual harassment. Those workers who were not Chicanas, the Russian Jews, lived in Boyle Heights in East Los Angeles. The two ethnic groups lived on separate blocks but met at the same streetcar stops in the early morning.

A booklet published by the International Ladies' Garment Workers' Union in 1934. As members of a union, women workers depended on each other as they tried to gain some control over their working conditions and wages.

Hispanic men and women join together for a 1935 meeting of the National Miners Union in Gallup, New Mexico.

Twenty-four-year-old Dorothy Ray Healey, an international vice president of the United Cannery, Agricultural, Packing and Allied Workers of America (UCAPAWA) and a cannery worker organizer since the age of 16, led the campaign. The strikers established a 24-hour picket line to demand that the company recognize their union and that all workers be union members.

Although the workers had walked out at the height of the peach-canning season, the factory owners, the Shapiros, refused to negotiate. Neighborhood grocers donated food to sustain the strikers. Many grocers refused to stock Cal San products. The National Labor Relations Board reprimanded the Shapiros for refusing to bargain, but the stalemate continued.

After two and a half months, one morning the Shapiros awoke in their comfortable house to an unusual sight. A small group of children in orderly picket lines on the Shapiros' well-manicured lawn carried signs saying "Shapiro is starving my Mama" and "I'm underfed because my Mama is underpaid." Surprised and moved, many of the Shapiros' neighbors brought the young picketers food, and several members of the Shapiros' synagogue reproached them. Finally the Shapiros agreed to meet with the union representatives.

The cannery workers' success had hinged on a strategy of incorporating women workers as parts of entire kinship and friendship networks, rather than as isolated individuals. In that way, the union represented these women's own sense of themselves as whole people. Unlike many relief and welfare policies, it did not force them to choose between being workers or wives, daughters or mothers.

For women textile workers too, the boundary between "mother" and "worker" was fuzzy. By 1940, 72 percent of the women workers in North Carolina's textile mills were married, up from less than half 10 years earlier. To these women, having a working husband was no guarantee of security. Even if a man neither drank nor gambled away his earnings he could fall ill, and in this delicately balanced economy every cent was essential. One unemployed widow told the editor of the Greenville, North Carolina, *News* that she valued the security that came from knowing she herself was a good mill hand. What she and other women wanted was not a handout, but "a chance to earn our bread." Laid off for their inability to match the speedup of machinery or by reduced mill hours, these women wanted work, not welfare or charity.

In the South, as in the West, some new unions attempted to organize across racial lines. White textile worker Eula McGill told an interviewer how her supervisor had laughed at her in 1934 when he found out she was helping to organize a union in Birmingham, Alabama. "'Hey,'" he said, "'you going to get Rosa into the union?' And I said, 'Yes, if she'll join.' (She was one of the black women who worked there—and they made less than we did.) He said, 'You going to call her sister?' I said, 'Sure I'm going to call her sister. I work with her, don't I?'"

Sometimes they tried more than they succeeded. When the Tobacco Workers International Union (TWIU) won a major strike in Durham, North Carolina, against Liggett & Myers in 1939, the union readily sacrificed black women workers to secure their contract. They allowed the company to mechanize the stemming department swiftly and to fire the large number of black women who worked there.

But some unions went in the other direction. The ILGWU had excluded black women from its Boston union as recently as 1933, and a victorious strike there had put black presser Mary Sweet out

A South Carolina mill worker in the 1930s. Most textile workers were married women who could not afford to depend solely on their husbands.

Chinese garment workers picket in San Francisco in 1938. The CIO, which organized workers by industry, proved far more inclusive than the AFL, and struggled to organize workers across divides of race as well as skill.

of work. However, a coalition of unions in New York City had created the Negro Labor Committee to advance the condition of black workers, and in 1934 the ILGWU asked Sweet to help them organize black women into the union. By the end of the year, ILGWU locals—not only in Boston but in New York, Chicago, and Philadelphia—included black women, and some had black officers. The union wage scale made some black garment workers among the best-paid women in Harlem, earning $45 to $50 for a 35-hour week.

Still, the cavalier treatment of black women by many organizations dominated by white men and women contributed to the special allure of the Communist party for black women and men in the 1930s. The Communist party (CP), more than any other organization in the decade, outspokenly supported black civil rights. Even the NAACP recognized by mid-decade that it was losing its role as primary civil rights advocate to the CP. The CP also paid at least lip service to equality between men and women. And in the South, it created organizations where whites and blacks worked together.

Both whites and blacks in the CP came from a variety of backgrounds. Mary Leonard, the widow of an Alabama druggist, had a solidly working-class background, but through her speaking abilities and her base of support among poor white housewives she became a party leader. Jane Speed was more demure in appearance than Leonard. Born into a wealthy southern family and educated in Austria, where she and her mother picked up left-wing sympathies, she appeared refined and unthreatening.

Among the African-American women in the party, Estelle Milner, daughter of an Alabama sharecropper, played a vital part as a young schoolteacher in linking black farmers to Communist leaders in Birmingham, Alabama. And Eula Gray, who at age 19 in 1931 held together the Communist-aided interracial Sharecroppers' Union and spurred the organization of 28 locals and 12 women's auxiliaries, came from a long line of black Alabama militants. Her great-grandfather had been a state legislator shortly after the Civil War. Her uncle Ralph, an independent farmer, was assassinated by white officials in 1931 for his role in organizing sharecroppers, and her father continued to risk his life for the same cause.

Sharecroppers picking cotton in Georgia. Both male and female members of the Sharecroppers Union shared the business of organizing, but they met separately so that one parent would always be home with the children.

The women's auxiliaries met separately from the men in the Sharecroppers Union, both so that one parent could always stay home with the children and to divert the suspicions of local white authorities, who were hostile to this attempt on the part of sharecroppers to drive a better bargain. But the women involved themselves as intimately as the men in the main business of the union. They read the Communist newspapers and kept up a correspondence that linked them to the national and international Communist movement. Like many neighborhood women who organized in the 1930s, they emphasized their need to feed and care for their families and their inability to do so under current conditions.

Perhaps the most telling protests of the decade, the ones that brought together the threads of women's roles, the New Deal, and worker relations, were the protests by WPA sewing project workers in 1939. In that year, Congress passed a relief appropriations act, the Woodrum Act, which cut WPA programs in half by revising eligibility requirements for WPA employment. Among other groups, the act barred workers who could receive Aid to Dependent Children (ADC).

In Minneapolis, WPA officials dismissed 900 women workers in early 1939, assuming they were eligible for ADC. Even if these women had been eligible, they would first have had to have ADC

A WPA sewing room in Tampa, Florida. In 1939, the WPA decided that women who could receive relief from the Aid to Dependent Children program could not qualify for WPA employment. Women sewers, however, depended on their WPA jobs and went on strike to protest the policy.

interviews and then await processing before they would receive any money, and the process was delayed because other people had recently been transferred into the system. Moreover, even if these women had ultimately gotten ADC, after weeks or months of no income, ADC still paid less than the WPA's work relief.

Many of the remaining women working in the sewing project, who were the chief support of their families, viewed themselves as the prime targets of the policy. WPA cuts continued into the spring. In May, 1,500 WPA workers voted to take a one-day holiday to protest the cuts. They formulated demands for the reinstatement of laid-off workers and an increase in relief work budgets, and they planned a march for June 2. On that day, more than 5,000 workers gathered in front of the Minneapolis WPA office. Yet on July 5 there were more layoffs and wage cuts. Workers on the Minneapolis state fairgrounds put down their tools and drove from one WPA project to the next, urging a general WPA strike. The next day, 8,000 Minneapolis workers stayed away from work, nearly closing all of the city's projects, and joining almost 125,000 relief workers on strike across the country.

After three days, the mayor of Minneapolis ordered police to go to the north Minneapolis sewing project, where fights began between women strikers and those women who continued to work. Despite a police escort through the strikers' lines, striking women harassed the non-strikers. They pulled hair and called out foul names.

Minnie Kohn, the organizer of one of the picket lines, took a different tack. A squad of women strikers rushed the entering women workers and tore their clothes off. As one witness told the press, "It was quite a sight. The strike-breakers naked amidst the jeers of the strikers."

Even this tactic failed. On July 21 the WPA workers agreed to end the strike, having made no gains. Strikers who had missed more than five days of work were fired. At least 160 people, about one-third of them women, were brought to trial on charges of conspiracy to intimidate relief clients, a felony under the Woodrum Act. Like Minnie Kohn, most of the women indicted had worked on the WPA project and were more than 50 years old. Some were self-supporting single women, and many others had families dependent on their WPA wage. Normally, they would have fit perfectly the image of crusading motherhood, as defenders of hearth and home. Instead, by taking matters into their own hands they threatened the New Deal image of women as helpless victims needing assistance.

At the trial, the attorneys and the press portrayed Kohn and her allies either as self-seeking individuals who had misled their followers (the prosecution's view) or as the victims not of job cuts but of jealous coworkers (the defense view). In neither case were they presented as working women defending their right to jobs because of their need to feed themselves and others. Minnie Kohn was sentenced to 45 days in the workhouse. The self-expressions of militant women workers had not succeeded in altering the dominant stereotypes of women or the policies based on them.

Willye Jeffries, Connie Smith, Eula McGill, Eula Gray, Minnie Kohn, and the others had refused to accept invisibility as their fate. They had taken matters into their own hands, including the matter of what it meant to be a woman struggling to survive in the 1930s. They rejected New Deal distinctions between women as workers and women as mothers, and they drew support from networks that related instead of separated neighborhood and workplace. These women met with many defeats, but they did enjoy some successes. Evictions were postponed. Wages were raised. And perhaps most important of all, women workers had made themselves seen and heard.

NEW JOBS FOR WOMEN

Everyone is getting used to 'overalled' women in machine shops

Women have made good as Street Car Conductors and Elevator Operators

Clerical Work quite a new job for Negro Girls

Slav, Italian and Negro Women making bed springs

The war brought us Women Traffic Cops and Mail Carriers

Laundry and domestic work didn't pay so they entered the garment trade

EPILOGUE

CHAPTER 9

F
ew decades have posed such vivid contrasts in the popular imagination as the Roaring Twenties and the dire thirties. For many women, however, that distinction never rang true. Many impoverished women on farms, such as Margaret Hagood's Mollie, saw little difference in their lives when economic hard times finally hit the rest of the country. For many other women—black and Chicana field and domestic workers, for example—the thirties were certainly dire, but the twenties had been no picnic.

For most women, however, even those not particularly prosperous, the 1920s had held out the promise of an easier life—appliances that would banish housework, canned food that made cooking quick, cars that opened new vistas of mobility. And the decade's "New Women" had the liberty to see themselves as first-class citizens.

Even before the Great Depression, the 1920s was having trouble making good on the decade's promises. The right to vote gave women few political offices. Women flocked to the workplace, but most ended up in a narrow range of jobs. Unexpected losses, such as limiting the number of women medical students, accompanied the gains. And the tensions between women's new opportunities and old definitions of family had led to a rising divorce rate. When the depression began, the country was already full of people worried about the family.

A federal government publication illustrates the progress of women's employment in the mid-20th century.

A pamphlet published by the Birth Control Clincial Research Bureau in 1938. By that time, the idea of woman as mother and wife was more prominent than the image of the independent flapper.

For the first time, in the 1930s, women gained significant policy influence in the federal government. The women who gained it had largely been career women in the 1920s, and often married career women at that. Many embodied the successful "New Woman." But they also personified an older split among active women.

During the final campaign for suffrage, some women had argued for the vote as a basic human right. Others had campaigned for the vote as a tool of social reform and had seen women as particularly concerned with social welfare as an answer to a chaotic society. By 1940, this split had not been resolved. In the 1920s, "New Women" had wanted their rights as individuals, not as women. In the 1930s, New Deal women entered politics to serve all of society and saw little distinct about women's needs. Yet in both decades—in the law, in government policy, in unions, in charities, and in the home—women had continued to be treated differently from men.

For many women, the 1920s could in some sense be seen as a time of rejecting the idea of "woman" *as* woman, in favor of searching for woman as individual. In the 1930s, the trend for women reversed; individualism was rejected in favor of embracing women in their family roles. Together, the two decades demonstrated the tension that had existed in the women's movement ever since its organized inception after the Civil War, without resolving it. And this era demonstrated the price that tension exacted in the lives of women on the breadlines. The determination to separate women's family roles from their economic roles had left the bulk of the country's women marooned when the depression swamped the nation. When women workers tried to take matters into their own hands and blend their work and family identities and responsibilities, they ran headlong into a void. By insisting on exposing those connections, however, they also created a set of possibilities for the future.

CHRONOLOGY

1917-18	United States involved in World War I
1920	Woman Suffrage Amendment (19th Amendment) ratified
1923	In *Adkins* v. *Children's Hospital,* the Supreme Court rules against minimum wage laws for women
1923	Equal Rights Amendment proposed
1929	North Carolina textile workers strike
1929	Stock market crashes
1932	Franklin Delano Roosevelt elected President
1933	New Deal starts; Frances Perkins appointed Secretary of Labor, first woman cabinet member
1935	Social Security Act provides aid to families with dependent children
1937	Mary McLeod Bethune heads Negro Division of National Youth Administration

FURTHER READING

A Note on Sources

In the interest of readability, the volumes in this series include no discussion of historiography and no footnotes. As works of synthesis and overview, however, they are greatly indebted to the research and writing of other historians. The principal works drawn on in this volume are among the books listed below.

Acosta-Belen, Edna, ed. *The Puerto Rican Woman: Perspectives on Culture, History and Society.* New York: Praeger, 1986.

Agee, James, and Walker Evans. *Let Us Now Praise Famous Men.* Boston: Houghton Mifflin, 1941.

Chafe, William. *Paradox of Change: American Women in the Twentieth Century.* New York: Oxford University Press, 1991.

Chesler, Ellen. *Woman of Valor: Margaret Sanger and the Birth Control Movement in America.* New York: Doubleday, 1993.

Cook, Blanche Wiesen. *Eleanor Roosevelt.* Vol. 1. New York: Viking, 1992.

Evans, Sarah M. *Born for Liberty: A History of Women in America.* New York: Free Press, 1989.

Faderman, Lillian. *Odd Girls and Twilight Lovers: A History of Lesbian Life in Twentieth-Century America.* New York: Viking Penguin, 1992.

Giddings, Paula. *When and Where I Entered: The Impact of Black Women on Race and Sex in America.* New York: Bantam, 1984.

Gordon, Linda. *Woman's Body, Woman's Right: Birth Control in America.* New York: Penguin, 1974.

Hagood, Margaret. *Mothers of the South: Portraiture of the White Tenant Farm Woman.* New York: Norton, 1977.

Jones, Jacqueline. *Labor of Love, Labor of Sorrow: Black Women, Work, and the Family from Slavery to the Present.* New York: Basic Books, 1985.

Leuchtenburg, William. *The Perils of Prosperity: 1914—1932.* Chicago: University of Chicago Press, 1958.

Low, Marie Ann. *Dust Bowl Diary.* Lincoln: University of Nebraska Press, 1984.

Lynd, Robert, and Helen Lynd. *Middletown.* New York: Harcourt, Brace & World, 1929.

McElvaine, Robert. *The Great Depression, America, 1929–1941.* New York: Times Books, 1984.

Mead, Margaret. *Blackberry Winter.* Magnolia, Mass.: Peter Smith, n.d.

O'Connor, Carol. *A Sort of Utopia: Scarsdale, 1891–1981.* Albany: State University of New York Press, 1983.

Qoyawayma, Polingaysi. *No Turning Back: A True Account of a Hopi Indian's Struggle to Bridge the Gap Between the World of Her People and the World of the White Man.* Albuquerque: University of New Mexico Press, 1964.

Roosevelt, Eleanor. *The Autobiography of Eleanor Roosevelt.* New York: Da Capo Press, 1992.

Ruiz, Vicki. *Cannery Women/ Cannery Lives: Mexican Women, Unionization, and the California Food Processing Industry, 1930–1950.* Albuquerque: University of New Mexico Press, 1987.

Showalter, Elaine, ed. *These Modern Women: Autobiographical Essays from the Twenties.* Old Westbury, N.Y.: Feminist Press, 1978.

Terkel, Studs. *Hard Times: An Oral History of the Great Depression in America.* New York: Pantheon, 1986.

Ware, Susan. *Beyond Suffrage: Women in the New Deal.* Cambridge: Harvard University Press, 1981.

———. *Partner and I: Molly Dewson, Feminism, and New Deal Politics.* New Haven: Yale University Press, 1987.

INDEX

Acknowledgments

Without the help of Melissa Walker's creative, energetic, and meticulous research this book could not have been completed on time. I am also grateful for the honest and intelligent feedback from my Clark University History 218 class on the U.S. in the Twenties and Thirties.

Picture Credits

Archives of Industrial Society, Hillman Library, University of Pittsburgh: 34-T, 34-B, 85-R, 102-R, 102-L, 124-R, 127; Archives of Labor and Urban Affairs, Wayne State University: 14-L, 14-R, 53; Atlanta History Center: 31, 113-L; Author's photos: 4, 66; Ball State University, A.M. Bracken Library, Archives and Special Collections: 28; Bethune Museum and Archives, Washington, D.C.: 107; California State University, Northridge, Urban Archives Center: 30; From *The Chicago Defender,* Feb. 18, 1928: 79; Chicago Historical Society: 17-L, 17-R; The Cincinnati Historical Society: 15, 16, 38-R, 87-T; Courtesy Clark University Archives: 47-B; Denver Public Library, Western History Department: 113-R; Department of Justice, Washington, D.C.: 120; Douglas County Museum photograph, Roseburg, Oregon: 24; Evanston Historical Society, Evanston, Illinois: 35; Florida State Archives: 25-B, 36, 45-R, 77, 95, 132; Hearst Newspaper Collection, Special Collections, University of Southern California Library: 39; Courtesy The Historic New Orleans Collection, Acc. No. 1981.324.2.202: 93; Jewish Historical Society of Southern California: 84; The Kansas State Historical Society, Topeka, Kansas: 43, 116; Library of Congress: frontispiece, 7, 10, 25-T, 26, 42, 46, 48, 54, 56, 59-R, 72, 76, 85-L, 89, 105, 109, 115, 118, 123, 126; Library of Congress/Courtesy Institute for Intercultural Studies, Inc., New York: 70; Library of Congress/Federal Theatre Project Collection at George Mason University, Fairfax, Virginia: 98; Minnesota Historical Society: 13; Missouri Historical Society: 82; Moorland Spingarn Research Center, Howard University: 124-L; Museum of Modern Art/Film Stills Archive: 57, 96; Courtesy Museum of New Mexico: 111, 114; National Archives: 58, 101, 125, 134; Collection of The New-York Historical Society: 131; New York Public Library, General Research Division, Astor, Lenox, and Tilden Foundations: 19, 59-L; Princeton University Libraries, Department of Rare Books and Special Collections: 73; San Francisco State University, Labor Archives and Research Center: 130; Courtesy Scarsdale Public Library, Scarsdale, New York: 62; Courtesy Scarsdale Public Library, Scarsdale, New York/photo by Ira N. Toff: 63; Schlesinger Library, Radcliffe College: 18, 20, 27, 29, 32, 47-T, 103; Schomburg Center for Research in Black Culture, The New York Public Library, Astor, Lenox, and Tilden Foundations: 75; Smith College Archives: 68; Smithsonian Institution: 8, 22, 38-L, 65, 78, 128; Sophia Smith Collection, Smith College: 61, 67, 90, 92, 136; South Caroliniana Library, University of South Carolina: 80, 129; State Historical Society of Wisconsin: 40, 122; Studio Museum in Harlem Archives/James Van Der Zee Collection: 74; UPI/Acme: 100; UPI/Bettmann: 97, 106; U.S. Department of Labor: 104; University of North Carolina at Chapel Hill, Southern Historical Collection: 52; University of Texas, The Institute of Texan Cultures, *The San Antonio Light* Collection: 49; Virginia State Library and Archives: 45-L, 50, 51, 88-T, 88-B; Wheatley Press: 110; Raphael Soyer. *Office Girls* (detail), 1936, oil on canvas, 26 x 24 inches. Collection of Whitney Museum of American Art, New York. Purchase 36.149: half-title page; Isaac Soyer. *Employment Agency* (1937), oil on canvas, 34 1/4 x 45 inches. Collection of Whitney Museum of American Art, New York. Purchase 37.44: 86.

Sarah Jane Deutsch is associate professor of history at Clark University, where she was awarded the Oliver and Dorothy Hayden Junior Faculty Fellowship for excellence in research and teaching. She is the author of *No Separate Refuge: Culture, Class, and Gender on an Anglo-Hispanic Frontier in the American Southwest, 1880–1940,* which won the Gustave O. Arlt Award in the Humanities from the Council of Graduate Schools, and the forthcoming *Women of Boston: Gender and the City, 1870–1950.* Professor Deutsch has worked with the Worcester, Massachusetts, public schools to introduce cultural and racial diversity into the U.S. history curriculum. She previously taught at Yale University and M.I.T. She holds a B.A. and Ph.D. from Yale and an M.Litt from Oxford University, where she was a Rhodes scholar.

Nancy F. Cott is Stanley Woodward Professor of history and American studies at Yale University. She is the author of *The Bonds of Womanhood: "Woman's Sphere" in New England 1780–1835, The Grounding of Modern Feminism,* and *A Woman Making History: Mary Ritter Beard Through Her Letters;* editor of *Root of Bitterness: Documents of the Social History of American Women;* and co-editor of *A Heritage of Her Own: Toward a New Social History of American Women.*